QUICK AND EASY
NOVELTY CAKES

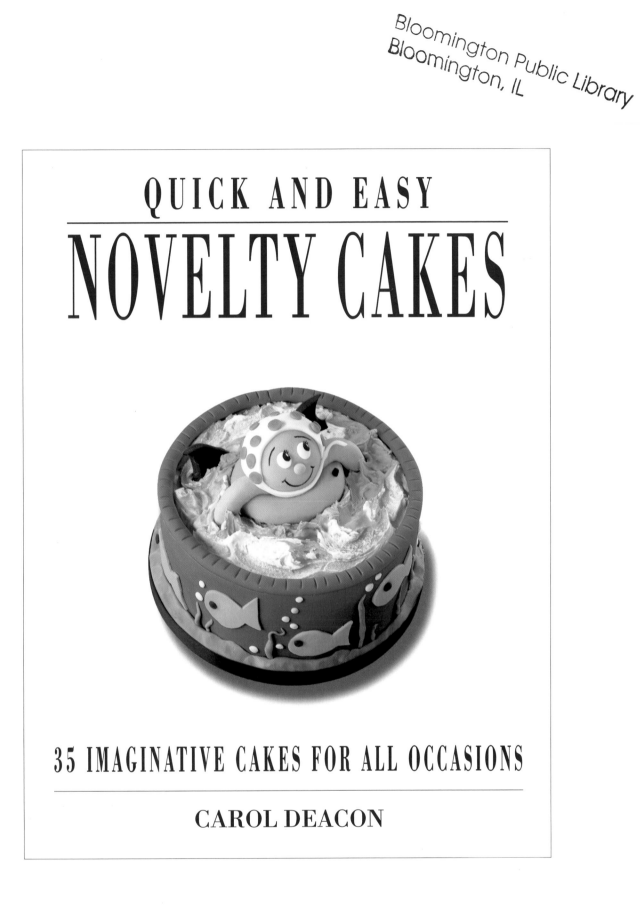

35 IMAGINATIVE CAKES FOR ALL OCCASIONS

CAROL DEACON

NEW
HOLLAND

To Chris for all your support and for putting up with all the mess!

First published in the UK in 1996 by
New Holland (Publishers) Ltd
London • Cape Town • Sydney • Singapore

24 Nutford Place
London W1H 6DQ
UK

P.O. Box 1144
Cape Town 8000
South Africa

3/2 Aquatic Drive
Frenchs Forest, NSW 2086
Australia

ISBN 1 85368 678 6 (hb)
ISBN 1 85368 735 9 (pb)

Managing Editor: Gillian Haslam
Editor: Caroline Plaisted
Designer: Paul Cooper
Photographer: Edward Allwright

Reproduction by Hirt and Carter (Pty) Ltd
Printed and bound in Malaysia

The author and publishers would like to thank J F Renshaw Ltd for supplying
sugarpaste, Cake Art Ltd for equipment, Craig Millar for cake mix, and
Divertimenti for the loan of kitchen equipment on pages 12 and 13.

CONTENTS

INTRODUCTION

I blame my friend Sally. In a rash moment, I had offered to make her a birthday cake, thinking that as her school nickname had been Frog, a plastic amphibian on top of something with a bow around the side would do the job perfectly. However, after a trip to a local cake baker's equipment shop, a whole new world had opened up: I had discovered sugar.

Not one to do things by halves, I jumped straight in and a rather bemused Sally became the recipient of a teeming frog pond, lavishly decorated with lily leaves, frogs and very watery water. (I hadn't quite conquered royal icing at that point!) Despite the wobbly piping, the odd dent and air bubble and the fact that she had to spend the entire party explaining the relevance of the frogs and reviving a nickname she thought she had left behind, she was thrilled and I was hooked.

It is the opportunity to make a cake completely individual and relevant for each person that really appeals to me. In this book, I have tried to cover as many hobbies, situations and special occasions as I could in the hope that you'll pick up the book, spot something and think 'hmm... now that would make the ideal cake for Aunty Mabel'.

As well as appealing to people with a bit of experience with sugarpaste, I hope this book will encourage those who have never tried cake decorating before to have a go. I have deliberately tried to avoid using any expensive bits of equipment – apart from the odd piping nozzle (tip) and cake smoothers (although someone once told me that a couple of cut up plastic lids work just as well), a heart-shaped cutter is about as exotic as it gets! I have also offered suggestions about to how to cheat wherever I can.

I really hope that this book inspires you to go forth and decorate!

Carol Deacon

P.S. Sally — if you want to make your own frog pond, the recipe's on page 60.

BASIC RECIPES

The cake you choose to make will depend on the recipient – and so too will the basic cake mixture. Here are three of the most popular cakes which should suit most tastes.

Madeira Cake

This extremely quick and easy recipe produces a firm-yet-moist cake that is ideal for carving into irregular shapes.

Square Tin (pan)		15 cm (6 in)	18 cm (7 in)	20 cm (8 in)	25 cm (10 in)
Round Tin (pan)	15 cm (6 in)	18 cm (7 in)	20 cm (8 in)	23 cm (9 in)	
Plain (All-purpose) Flour	175g (6 oz/1 ½ cups)	225 g (8 oz/2 cups)	350 g (12 oz/2 ½ cups)	450 g (1 lb/4 cups)	600 g (1 lb 5 oz/5 ¼ cups)
Baking Powder	4 ml (¾ tsp)	5 ml (1 tsp)	7.5 ml (1 ½ tsp)	10 ml (2 tsp)	15 ml (3 tsp)
Caster (Superfine) Sugar	100 g (4 oz/½ cup)	175 g (6 oz/¾ cup)	275 g (10 oz/1 ¼ cups)	400 g (14 oz/1 ¾ cups)	500 g (1 lb 2 oz/2 ¼ cups)
Soft Margarine	100 g (4 oz/½ cup)	175 g (6 oz/¾ cup)	275 g (10 oz/1 ¼ cups)	400 g (14 oz/1 ¾ cups)	500 g (1 lb 2 oz/2 ¼ cups)
Eggs (No 3/Large)	2	3	5	7	9
Milk	15 ml (1 tbsp)	30 ml (2 tbsp)	45 ml (3 tbsp)	52 ml (3 ½ tbsp)	75 ml (5 tbsp)
Baking Time (approx)	1-1 ¼ hrs	1 ¼-1 ½ hrs	1 ½-1 ¾ hrs	1 ¾-2 hrs	1 ¾-2 hrs

1 Pre-heat the oven to 160°C/325°F/Gas 3. Grease and line a cake tin (pan).
2 Sift the flour and baking powder into a bowl. Add all the other ingredients and mix together. Beat together with an electric whisk (mixer) at a fairly high speed for one minute or until the mixture (batter) is smooth.
3 Place the mixture into a tin that has been lined with greaseproof paper. Smooth the top with a spatula.
4 Place the tin into the centre of the oven and bake for the specified time according to the size of the tin. Test to see that the cake is baked by lightly pressing the centre. If it springs back and is a golden brown colour then it should be cooked. Wait for about five minutes before turning the cake out. Peel off the paper and leave to cool on a wire rack.

Chocolate Cake

The most important part of this recipe is to make sure that you use a good strong plain chocolate with at least 70% cocoa solids. Don't be tempted by cheaper blocks of cooking chocolate because it just won't produce the same quality of taste. There's nothing more disappointing than biting into a luscious lump of chocolate cake and finding a synthetic fraud lurking inside. This recipe produces a cake that is moist and firm with a wonderful velvety texture. It has completely won over all the chocoholics I know!

Square Tin (pan)		15 cm (6 in)	18 cm (7 in)	20 cm (8 in)
Round Tin (pan)	15 cm (6 in)	18 cm (7 in)	20 cm (8 in)	23 cm (9 in)
Butter	75g (3 oz/6 tbsp)	100 g (4 oz/½ cup)	175 g (6 oz/¾ cup)	225 g (8 oz/1 cup)
Caster (Superfine) Sugar	40 g (1 ½ oz/3 ½ tbsp)	65 g (2 ½ oz/5 ½ tbsp)	100 g (4 oz/½ cup)	150 g (5 oz/¾ cup)
Eggs (No 3/Large), separated	3	4	6	8
Plain (Semisweet) Chocolate	150 g (5 oz)	175 g (6 oz)	225 g (8 oz)	275 g (10 oz)
Icing (Confectioners') Sugar	25 g (1 oz/¼ cup)	25 g (1 oz/1 cup)	50 g (2 oz/1 ½ cups)	75 g (3 oz/2 cups)
Self-Raising (Self-Rising) Flour	75 g (3 oz/¾ cup)	100 g (4 oz/1 cup)	175 g (6 oz/1 ½ cups)	225 g (8 oz/2 cups)
Baking Time (approx)	45 mins-1 hr	45 mins-1 hr	1-1 ¼ hrs	1- 1 ¼ hrs

1 Pre-heat the oven to 180°C/350°F/Gas 4. Grease and line a cake tin (pan) and melt the chocolate.
2 Cream the butter and sugar until light and fluffy.
3 Gradually beat in the egg yolks and then add the chocolate.

4 In a separate bowl, whisk (beat) the egg whites to form soft peaks.
5 Gradually whisk the icing (confectioners') sugar into the whites.
6 Sift the flour and then, using a large metal spoon, fold the flour alternately with the egg whites into the chocolate mixture.
7 Spoon the mixture into the prepared tin and bake for the required time. Wait five minutes before turning the cake out.

As it bakes, a crust will form on top of the cake making it difficult to tell whether it's baked by touch alone. So insert a skewer or knife. If it comes out clean, the cake is ready. If it doesn't, bake for a little longer. When it's baked, turn out the cake immediately. Peel off the lining paper and allow to cool on a wire rack. Cut off and discard the crust before decorating.

Fruit Cake

Because it takes such a long time for a fruit cake to bake right through, it really is worth spending time preparing the tin (pan) beforehand. By double lining the sides and base with greaseproof (waxed) paper and wrapping a double layer of brown paper (or a brown paper bag) secured with string around the outside, you will greatly reduce any risk of the outside of the cake browning before the inside is baked. Fifteen minutes before the end of the suggested baking time test the cake to see if it is baked through. Insert a skewer. If it comes out clean, the cake is baked. If not, place the cake back in the oven and test again at 15 minute intervals.

Square Tin (pan)	15 cm (6 in)	18 cm (7 in)	30 cm (12 in)
Currants	150 g (5 oz/1 cup)	175 g (6 oz/1 heaped cup)	750 g (1 ½ lb/4 ½ cups)
Sultanas (Golden Raisins)	150 g (5 oz/1 cup)	175 g (6 oz/1 heaped cup)	750 g (1 ½ lb/4 ½ cups)
Raisins	150 g (5 oz/1 cup)	175 g (6 oz/1 heaped cup)	750 g (1 ½ lb/4 ½ cups)
Mixed Peel	25 g (1 oz/¼ cup)	40 g (1 ½ oz/3 tbsp)	175 g (6 oz/1 ½ cups)
Halved Glacé Cherries	50 g (2 oz/⅓ cup)	65 g (2 ½ oz/heaped ½ cup)	225 g (8 oz/1 ½ cups)
Brandy	30 ml (2 tbsp)	45 ml (3 tbsp)	105 ml (7 tbsp)
Butter	150 g (5 oz/10 tbsp)	175 g (6 oz/¾ cup)	750 g (1 ½ lb/3 cups)
Soft Dark Brown Sugar	150 g (5 oz/1 cup packed)	175 g (6 oz/1 heaped cup)	750 g (1 ½ lb/6 cups)
Black Treacle (Molasses), optional	12.5 ml (¾ tbsp)	15 ml (1 tbsp)	60 ml (4 tbsp)
Eggs (No 3/Large)	3	4	5
Plain (All-purpose) Flour	100 g (4 oz/1 cup)	165 g (5 ½ oz/1 ½ cups plus 2 tbsp)	500 g (1 lb 2 oz/4 ½ cups)
Mixed Spice (Apple Pie Spice)	10 g (¼ oz/2 tbsp)	12.5 g (¾ oz/2 ½ tbsp)	50 g (2 oz/4 tbsp)
Lemons (zest only)	1	1	3
Ground Almonds	25 g (1 oz/¼ cup)	40 g (1 ½ oz/⅓ cup)	175 g (6 oz/1 ½ cups)
Flaked (Slivered) Almonds	25 g (1 oz/¼ cup)	40 g (1 ½ oz/⅓ cup)	175 g (6 oz/1 ½ cups)
Cinnamon	10 g (¼ oz/2 tsp)	10 g (¼ oz/2 tsp)	25 g (1 oz/2 tsp)
Baking Time (approx)	2-2 ¼ hrs	2 ¼ -2 ½ hrs	3-3 ½ hrs

1 Pre-heat the oven to 150°C/300°F/Gas 2 and prepare the cake tin/pan (see recipe introduction).
2 Place all the dried fruits in a mixing bowl. Pour over the brandy. Stir, cover and allow to soak overnight.
3 Cream the butter and sugar together. Stir in the black treacle (molasses) if using.
4 Slowly beat in the eggs.
5 Mix in the sifted flour and spices. If the mixture still seems runny, add a little more flour.
6 Stir in the soaked fruits, lemon zest and almonds.

7 Spoon into the tin and bake for the required time. Allow the cake to cool completely in the tin before turning out and removing the paper. If you wish to store the cake, pierce the top with a cocktail stick (toothpick) a few times and drizzle a little brandy into the holes. Double wrap the cake first with a layer of greaseproof (waxed) paper and then tin (aluminium) foil and store in an airtight tin. 'Feed' with a little brandy at regular intervals (about once a week). The maximum storage time is about three months.

Stock Syrup

A secret method of ensuring that your sponge and chocolate cakes are always wonderfully moist even if you make them in advance.

Ingredients

100 g (4 oz/½ cup) granulated or caster (superfine) sugar
150 ml (¼ pint/⅔ cup) water

1 Place the sugar and water into a saucepan and bring to the boil.
2 Simmer for 2-3 minutes until the sugar has dissolved.
3 Allow to cool.
To use, simply 'paint' the syrup onto the layers of cake allowing it to soak in slightly. Don't saturate the cake. When you are ready, spread with buttercream and assemble the cake as usual. The syrup can also be flavoured with any spirit or liqueur.

Buttercream

Throughout the book I have tended to use buttercream to both fill and coat the cakes before covering with sugarpaste (rolled fondant icing). As you spread it over the sponge, it automatically fills in any holes or imperfections leaving you with a smoother surface to work with.

If you have time, place the cake into the refrigerator for an hour after it's been coated with buttercream. This will allow the buttercream to harden and make it less likely to collapse or for the buttercream to ooze out of the sides of the layers as it's being covered with sugarpaste. When you take the cake out of the fridge, spread another thin layer of buttercream over the top and sides to give the sugarpaste a good surface to adhere to.

Ingredients

250 g (10 oz/2 cups) unsalted butter, softened
500 g (1 lb 2 oz/4 ½ cups) icing (confectioners') sugar, sieved (sifted)
Few drops vanilla extract

1 Place the butter in a bowl and beat until light and fluffy.
2 Add the sugar and vanilla extract and continue to beat until the the mixture changes colour and becomes almost white. The buttercream can be flavoured with either melted plain (semisweet) chocolate, 1 tablespoon of cocoa mixed with 1 tablespoon of boiling water, 2 teaspoons of instant coffee mixed with 1 teaspoon of boiling water, orange or lemon rind (peel) or a few drops of flavoured essence (extract).

Royal Icing

Although traditional royal icing uses real egg whites, the use of uncooked egg is not recommended, because of the slight risk of food poisoning. Dried egg white is available from supermarkets, cake decorating equipment shops and mail-order suppliers and produces icing just as good as the real thing. The instructions here are for use with dried egg albumen (or meringue powder) which is available from specialist cake decorating shops and mail-order suppliers. Read the instructions on the side of the box before making up just in case the amounts differ slightly.

Ingredients

1 tbsp dried egg albumen (meringue powder)
5 tbsp water
500 g (1 lb 2 oz/4 ½ cups) icing (confectioners') sugar, sieved

1 Mix the albumen and water together and blend until smooth.
2 Place the icing sugar into a grease-free electric mixer bowl.
3 Tip in the egg mixture and beat on the lowest speed for about 5-10 minutes until the icing stands up in peaks.
4 Place the icing into a bowl with a tight-fitting lid, laying a strip of clingfilm (plastic wrap) directly on top of the icing.

Sugarpaste (Rolled Fondant Icing)

Because interest in sugarcraft (European-style cake decorating) has grown so much over the past few years, sugarpaste (rolled fondant icing) is now easily available from most supermarkets. There are several brands available and I suggest you try them out to see which one you prefer. If you can't find any at a supermarket, try a specialist mail-order supplier.

Although available in many colours, sugarpaste can easily be coloured using paste food colours. (Don't use the liquid food colours or the sugarpaste will become an unmanageable soggy mess.) Simply add the food colouring to the sugarpaste using a cocktail stick (toothpick) and knead it in. Always make any special colour-mixes before you start making the cake.

Just in case you have problems obtaining sugarpaste, I have included a simple recipe for a homemade version.

Ingredients

500 g (1 lb 2 oz/5 cups) icing (confectioners') sugar
1 egg white (or equivalent amount of dried egg albumen (meringue powder) mixed with water)
30 ml (2 tbsp) liquid glucose (available from chemists and drug stores as well as cake decoration equipment shops)

1 Place the icing sugar into a bowl and make a well in the centre.
2 Tip the egg white and liquid glucose into the well before stirring together with a wooden spoon.
3 Finish binding the paste together with your hands, kneading it until all the sugar is incorporated. The sugarpaste should feel silky and smooth.
4 Store immediately in a plastic bag.

Gelatin Icing

This is an extremely useful type of icing because it sets very hard. Shapes can be cut out of it and allowed to harden so that you can stand them up when dry or it can be moulded over things and left to take on the shape of an object.

Ingredients

60 ml (4 tbsp) water
15 g (½ oz) sachet (envelop) gelatin powder
10 ml (2 tsp) liquid glucose
500 g (1 lb 2 oz/5 cups) icing (confectioners') sugar, sifted
Cornflour (cornstarch)

1 Place the water into a small heatproof bowl and add the gelatin. Leave to soak for about two minutes.
2 Put about 1 cm (½ in) water into a saucepan. Stand the bowl in the water and heat gently until the gelatin dissolves.
3 Remove from the heat and stir in the liquid glucose. Allow to cool for a minute.
4 Place the icing (confectioners') sugar into a mixing bowl. Tip the gelatin mixture into the centre and mix in. Knead to a bread dough consistency adding cornflour (cornstarch) as required. Store in plastic bags or clingfilm (plastic wrap) until ready to use.

Coloured Sugar or Dessicated (Shredded) Coconut

Simply place the sugar (either caster/superfine or granulated) or coconut into a small bowl and add a small amount of food colour paste (not liquid). Stir in the colour, adding more if necessary until you achieve the desired shade.

BASIC TECHNIQUES

Whether you are covering the cake board or cleaning up sticky finger marks, perfecting your basic skills will make all the difference to the finished look of your cakes.

Covering Cakes

Always roll out the sugarpaste (rolled fondant icing) on a surface dusted with icing (confectioners') sugar to prevent it sticking. Roll the sugarpaste approximately 15 cm (6 in) larger than the top of the cake. Lift the icing and place it over the cake using a rolling pin if desired. Smooth over the top and sides with your hands and trim away any excess from the base (*fig 1*). A pair of cake smoothers (or firm metal spatula) is crucial for giving your cakes a neat, professional finish. Simply run them over the top and sides of the cake smoothing away any bumps, ridges or other imperfections, a bit like an iron (*fig 2*).

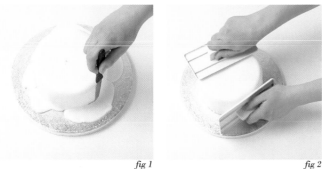

fig 1 *fig 2*

Covering the Cake Board

There are various ways to cover a cake board and the technique you use will depend on the style and design of your cake:

The Bandage Method

Place the cake onto the board and run a tape measure around the side of the cake to find the measurement of the exposed cake board. Cut out a strip of icing slightly wider than the board and about 3mm (⅛ in) thick. Roll it up like a bandage. Moisten the cake board with a little water and starting from the back of the cake, slowly unwind the 'bandage' allowing the icing to fall onto the board (*fig 3*). Run a cake smoother over the surface of the covered board and trim away the excess from the edges with a sharp knife.

fig 3

The Fabric Effect

This is an extremely useful method of covering a board. Not only is it easy and quick but it can also be used to disguise and hide imperfections because the icing rests against the side of the cake. Moisten the cake board with water. Roll sugarpaste (rolled fondant icing) out to a thickness of about 3 mm (⅛ in). Cut four strips wider and longer than the exposed board. Lay the sugarpaste onto the board, allowing it to fall into folds and creases as it lands on the board (*fig 4*). Use one strip per side. Run a knife around the edge of the board to trim away any excess. Press down any gaping holes at the edges with your thumb.

All-In-One

fig 4

This is probably the easiest method of all. Simply knead a ball of sugarpaste (rolled fondant icing) until pliable. Moisten the cake board with a little water and then roll out the sugarpaste into a flattish circle. Transfer the icing onto the centre of the board and continue to roll it out until it just goes over the edge of the board (*fig 5*). Run a cake smoother over the surface and trim away the excess from the edges with a sharp knife.

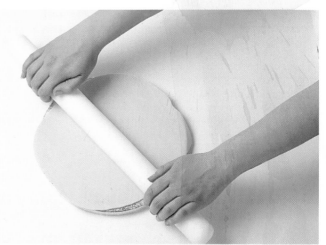

fig 5

fig 6

Covering a Board in Four Strips

This is a useful method for covering the board around a square or rectangular cake. Roll the sugarpaste (rolled fondant icing) out to a thickness of about 3 mm (⅛ in). Cut four strips slightly wider and longer than the sides of the exposed cake board. Moisten the board with a little water. Lay one strip along each side of the cake. Make a diagonal cut from the edge of the board to the edge of the cake at each corner. Lift up and peel away the excess icing at each corner so that the two edges should now lie neatly together. Run a sharp knife around the edges to trim away the excess (fig 6).

Covering the Board Around an Awkward-Shaped Cake

Although covering a board after the cake is in position might look more difficult than covering it all-in-one and placing the cake on top afterwards, it is easier than it looks and has one distinct advantage. Because you slide the sugarpaste (rolled fondant icing) up against the edge of the cake, it makes a neater join at the base of the cake. Moisten the cake board with a little water. Thinly roll out the sugarpaste and cover the exposed board in sections (fig 7). Run a cake smoother over the surface to flatten any lumps and trim away the excess from the edges using a sharp knife.

fig 7

Edging the Cake Board

You can neaten the outer edge of the cake board by sticking small strips of double-sided tape around the board and attaching ribbon to it.

Filling the Gap at the Base of a Cake

After neatening and levelling the top of a cake, turn it upside down on the cake board so that the base then forms a nice, flat top. This sometimes produces a gap between the outer edges of the cake and the board. If you're using sponge cake and the gap is not too large, then simply fill it with buttercream as you coat the outside.

If it is really noticeable then roll out a thin 'sausage' (rope) of icing. Flatten one edge with your finger and slide this into the gap (fig 8). Trim away the excess with a sharp knife.
The same procedure is also used on fruitcakes, although with marzipan (almond paste) instead of icing.

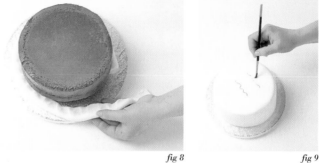

fig 8   fig 9

Cleaning Sugarpaste (rolled fondant icing)

Any mistakes made when painting with food colour (e.g. the mouth and eyelashes on the teddy bear cake) can easily be rectified. Gently rub the error with a paintbrush dipped in a little clean water, then wipe away using a clean damp cloth. Repeat until the area is clean (fig 9). Be careful not to make water splashes as any drips will begin to dissolve the surface of the sugarpaste (rolled fondant icing) leaving behind unsightly marks.

Making a Woodgrain Effect

This effective technique is easy to achieve. Roll a ball of white sugarpaste (rolled fondant icing) into a sausage (rope) shape and streak with dashes of different shades of brown food colour (e.g chestnut, dark brown and paprika) applied with a knife or cocktail stick (toothpick) (fig 10). Fold the rolled sugarpaste in half and roll together to form another sausage (fig 11). Fold in half and roll again, applying a little more food colour if necessary. Repeat until a good strong wood effect is clearly visible then roll it out as usual.

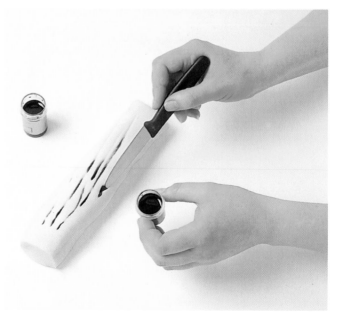

fig 10

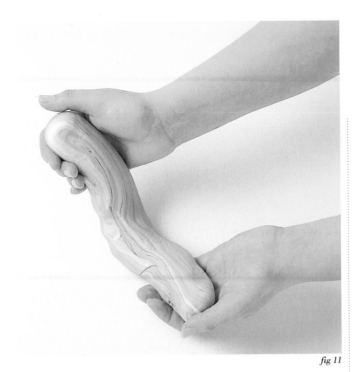

fig 11

Marbling Effect

This has got to be the simplest of all effects to achieve in sugarpaste (rolled fondant icing). Simply take a ball of white sugarpaste and partially knead in a small ball of a contrasting coloured icing or a few streaks of food colour (*fig 12*). If you go too far and the icing becomes all one colour, simply reverse the process by kneading in a little white. When you roll out the sugarpaste it will be marbled (*fig 13*).

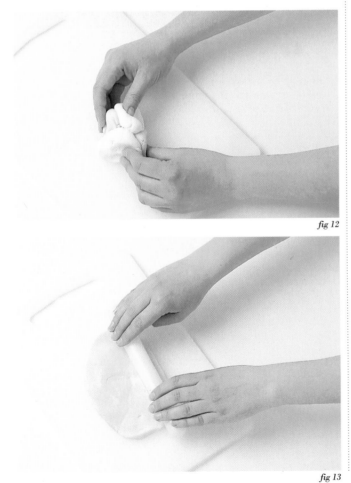

fig 12

fig 13

Making a Piping (Decorating) Bag

1 Cut some greaseproof (waxed) paper into a triangle.

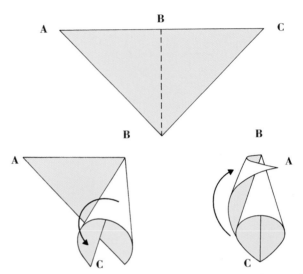

2 Pick up corner 'C' and fold over, so that 'B' forms a sharp cone in the centre.

3 Wrap corner 'A' around the cone.

4 Make sure that both 'A' and 'C' are at the back and that the point of the cone is sharp.

5 Fold points 'A' and 'C' inside the top edge of the bag to hold it firmly and securely. Snip of the end and insert a piping nozzle (tip).

Additional Hints and Tips

● A lot of the hard work can be taken out of kneading marzipan (almond paste) by heating it for a few seconds in a microwave. However, don't over do it or the oil in the centre of the marzipan will get very hot and can give you a nasty burn when you start to use it.

● After you've painstakingly covered your cake with sugarpaste (rolled fondant icing), you might find that an unsightly air bubble has appeared on the surface. Simply prick the bulge with a clean dressmaker's pin and gently press the area flat.

● Get rid of any dusty icing (confectioners') sugar marks after you have finished by wiping away with either a clean damp cloth or paintbrush. Be careful when cleaning dark colours such as red, black or dark green as they bleed easily.

● Clingfilm (plastic wrap) is an invaluable aid in cake decoration. Not only can it be used to wrap the sugarpaste (rolled fondant icing) but, scrunched up into a ball, it can act as a support for things that are drying.

EQUIPMENT

SIEVE (STRAINER) Vital for sifting flour and icing sugar. Also a useful tool for making bushes or hair by simply pushing a lump of sugarpaste (rolled fondant icing) through the mesh.

MIXING BOWLS Even the simplest cake uses more than one bowl, so a good selection of bowls is useful.

CAKE SMOOTHERS By using a smoother like an iron, and running it over the surface of a covered cake, small bumps and lumps can literally be ironed out. Essential for achieving a smooth professional finish.

MEASURING SPOONS A set of standard measuring spoons is useful as it ensures that you use the same quantities each time you re-make a recipe.

DRINKING STRAWS These can be used as tiny circle cutters and are ideal for making eyes. Held at an angle and pressed into sugarpaste, they can also be used for making the scales on dragons or snakes.

PIPING NOZZLES (TIPS) OR TUBES A varied selection is always useful and they can always double up as small circle cutters. Metal nozzles are more expensive than plastic but are sharper and more accurate.

COCKTAIL STICKS (TOOTHPICKS) They can be used as hidden supports inside models, for adding food colour to sugarpaste, and for making frills and dotty patterns.

TURNTABLE Although not strictly speaking essential, once you've used one, you'll wonder what you ever did without it. Cheaper versions are available in plastic.

RULER Not just for measuring, a ruler can also be useful for pressing lines and patterns into sugarpaste.

SCISSORS A decent pair of sharp scissors is essential for shaping ribbons, snipping the ends off piping bags, cutting linings for tins, and sometimes sugarpaste.

TAPE MEASURE Handy for measuring the circumference of cakes and boards to ensure that you have rolled out enough sugarpaste to go around.

COOLING RACK Available in all shapes and sizes, and used for cooling cakes.

SMALL DISHES Useful for holding water when modelling, icing sugar when rolling out sugarpaste. They also come into their own when mixing food colour into small quantities of royal icing.

BAKING TINS A good assortment of shapes and sizes is useful.

ROLLING PIN A long rolling pin like the one shown will not leave handle dents behind in the sugarpaste. Tiny ones are also available and are extremely handy for rolling out small quantities of sugarpaste when modelling. If you don't possess a small rolling pin, a paintbrush handle will often do the job just as well.

CUTTERS Although only basic holly, heart and circle cutters are shown here, a vast range is available in both plastic and metal.

SOFT PASTRY BRUSH It is useful to have two in your collection – one for dampening or cleaning large areas, the other for brushing away dusty fingerprints or small specks of dried sugarpaste.

PAINTBRUSHES A selection of various sizes is useful. A medium brush is good for sticking things with water when modelling, and a fine brush for adding delicate detail. Although more expensive, sable brushes are the best.

SCALPEL Invaluable when sharp, careful cutting is required such as when tracing around a template.

GREASEPROOF (WAXED) PAPER Used for lining tins, making piping bags, storing fruit cakes, and instead of tracing paper.

WOODEN SPOON As well as mixing, the handle can be used as a modelling tool for making folds.

PALETTE KNIFE (METAL SPATULA) For spreading jam or buttercream, mixing colour into larger quantities of royal icing, and lifting small bits of sugarpaste.

CARVING KNIFE A long, sharp serrated knife is essential for shaping and slicing cakes.

SMALL SHARP KNIFE A small kitchen knife with a sharp, straight blade will become one of your most important bits of equipment. Don't let anyone run off with it to peel the potatoes!

BOARD
Useful when modelling small items. Non-stick ones are also available.

Ruler

Measuring spoons

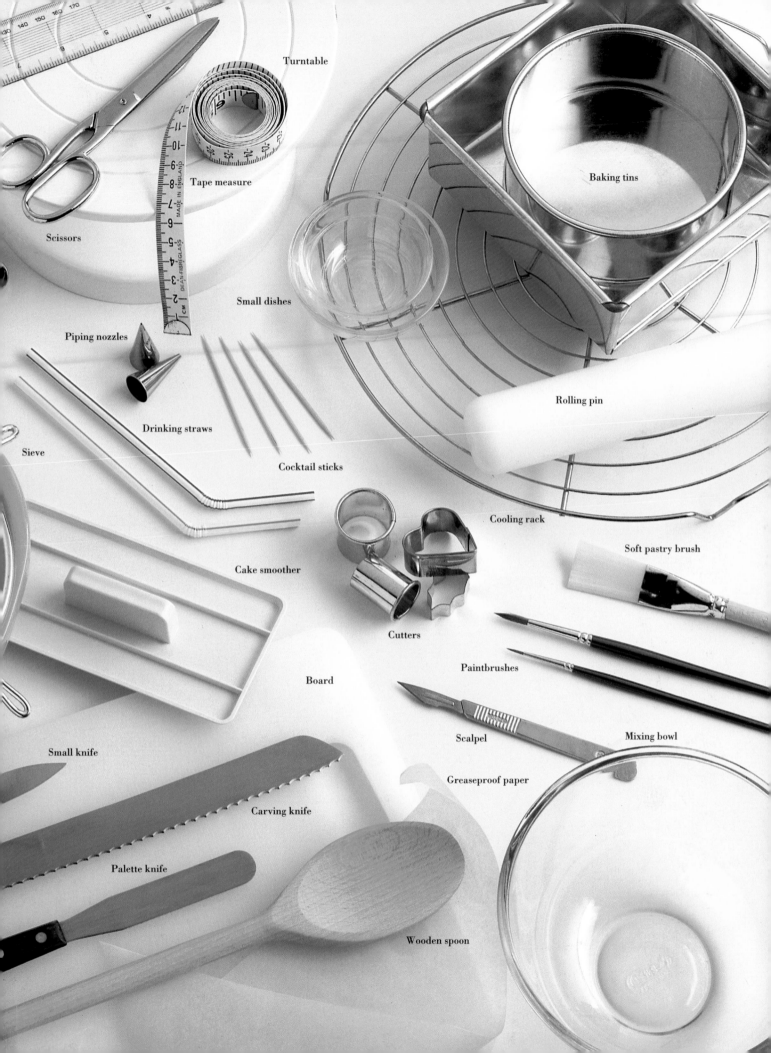

Turntable

Tape measure

Scissors

Baking tins

Small dishes

Piping nozzles

Drinking straws

Rolling pin

Sieve

Cocktail sticks

Cooling rack

Cake smoother

Soft pastry brush

Cutters

Paintbrushes

Board

Scalpel

Mixing bowl

Small knife

Greaseproof paper

Carving knife

Palette knife

Wooden spoon

CHILDREN'S CAKES

From man-eating dinosaurs, to burgers, rag dolls and U.F.O.s. There should be something amongst the sixteen designs featured in this section to appeal to most children. And if he's been a bit naughty, and doesn't really deserve a cake at all, you could always make him a 'Horrible Child'!

PADDLING POOL

From the complete novice to the keen swimmer, this is the ideal cake for any water baby, especially if they are about to enter a swimming competition. If you really want to make the cake a memorable one, stir a little blue food colour into the cake mix before cooking to add an extra blue surprise when the cake is cut.

INGREDIENTS

15 cm (6 in) round cake
1 quantity of buttercream (see page 10)
500 g (1 lb 2 oz) white sugarpaste (rolled fondant icing)
200 g (7 oz) orange sugarpaste (rolled fondant icing)
100 g (4 oz) flesh-coloured sugarpaste (rolled fondant icing)
100 g (4 oz) green sugarpaste (rolled fondant icing)
450 g (1 lb) dark blue sugarpaste (rolled fondant icing)
10 g (¼ oz) black sugarpaste (rolled fondant icing)
Black and blue food colours
3 tbsp royal icing (see page 10)
Icing (confectioners') sugar, for rolling out
Water

UTENSILS

20 cm (8 in) round cake board
Carving knife
Small sharp knife
Palette knife (metal spatula)
Rolling pin
Cake smoothers
No 3 piping nozzle (round tip)
Paintbrush
Small plastic bags

1 Level the cake if necessary and place upside down onto the cake board. Slice in half and fill the centre with buttercream. Then cover the top and sides with buttercream as well.

2 Cover the cake with the white sugarpaste (rolled fondant icing). Trim the edges and smooth the sides using smoothers. Keep the bits of excess white sugarpaste for the hat and bubbles later.

3 Now make the swimmer (*fig 1*). Mould 100 g (4 oz) of orange sugarpaste into a sausage about 18 cm (7 in) long. Moisten the ends and bend it round to form a doughnut shape. Make two arms out of 10 g (¼ oz) flesh-

fig 1

coloured sugarpaste by rolling out two small sausages (ropes) of about 5 cm (2 in) long. Flatten one end of each arm slightly and press this end over the top of the ring.

Roll 75 g (3 oz) of flesh-coloured sugarpaste into a ball to form the head. Lightly moisten the top of the rubber ring with a little water and carefully place the head on top of the arms.

Roll out 20 g (¾ oz) of white sugarpaste and cut out a semi-circle 9 cm (3 ½ in) wide to form the hat. Moisten the top of the head and fold the icing over the head. Cut a small

string of leftover icing and stick this under the head to make a strap. Press the tip of a No 3 piping nozzle (round tip) into one end of the strap to make a button.

Add two tiny flattened balls of white for eyes and a flesh-coloured ball for a nose. Paint in the eyeballs, eyelashes, eyebrows and mouth with black food colour and a fine paintbrush.

Stick small flattened balls of green icing onto the hat and a tiny black circle for a stopper onto the rubber ring.

4 Partially mix a small amount of blue food colour into the royal icing. Spread this around the top of the cake

with a small palette knife (metal spatula) (*fig 2*). Place the swimmer on top of the cake. Ease the icing into any awkward bits, such as under the arms, with a damp paintbrush.

fig 2

5 Knead and roll out about 375 g (13 oz) of blue sugarpaste to a thickness of 1 cm (½ in). Cut out a strip 55 cm x 7.5 cm (22 in x 3 in). Moisten the side of the cake. Roll the blue icing up like a bandage. Then, holding it upright, begin to unwind it around the cake starting from the back (*fig 3*). Press the ends together, applying a little water with a paintbrush if necessary. Add more royal icing if needed with a teaspoon and push it right to the edges of the pool.

Roll the remaining blue sugarpaste into a sausage about 60 cm (24 in) long. Moisten the top edge of the pool and lay it around the

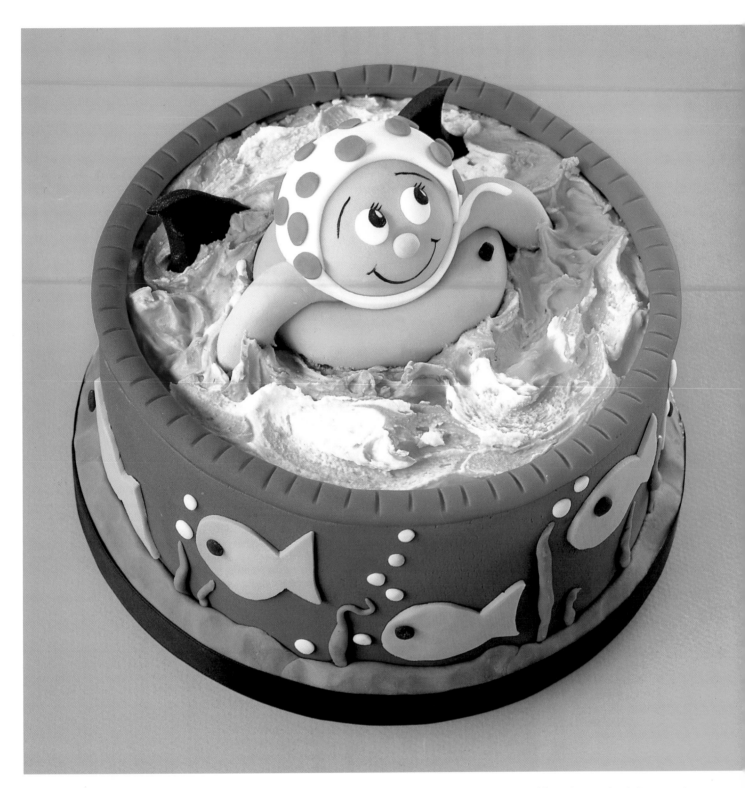

fig 3

edge. Press the blunt edge of a knife around the top to make a decorative pattern.

6 Wipe around the edge of the pool with a clean damp cloth to rid it of any dusty fingermarks.

7 Roll out the remaining orange sugarpaste and cut out ten simple fish shapes. Stick them around the pool.

8 Attach tiny strips of green sugarpaste up the side of the pool. Moisten the exposed cake board and press the rest of the green sugarpaste around the base.

9 Give the fish tiny flattened balls of black sugarpaste for eyes and add a few tiny flattened balls of white sugarpaste near the fish to look like air bubbles.

10 Make two shark fins out of black sugarpaste triangles with the top bent back slightly. Place in the water behind the swimmer.edge of a knife

TIP: *If the recipient of the cake is male, omit the bathing cap and add a small tuft of suitably coloured hair instead.*

BURGER

Even the most surly teenager whose favourite meal consists of burger and French fries and who insists that they're too old for a birthday cake should find this one amusing. (Unless they become worried that it will give them even more spots than they've already got!) See the tip for an easy adaptation.

INGREDIENTS

15 cm (6 in) round cake
1 quantity buttercream (see page 10)
800 g (12 oz) orangey-brown coloured sugarpaste (rolled fondant icing)
150 g (5 oz) green sugarpaste (rolled fondant icing)
300 g (11 oz) dark brown sugarpaste (rolled fondant icing)
250 g (9 oz) red sugarpaste (rolled fondant icing)
150 g (5 oz) yellow sugarpaste (rolled fondant icing)
25 g (1 oz) orange sugarpaste (rolled fondant icing)
Icing (confectioners') sugar, for rolling out
Water

UTENSILS

25 cm (10 in) round cake board
Carving knife
Small sharp knife
Palette knife
Rolling pin
Cake smoothers
Tin (aluminium) foil
Drinking straw
No 3 piping nozzle (round tip)
Fish slice (pancake turner)
Paintbrush
Small plastic bags

fig 1

1 Carefully carve the edges of the cake so that it forms a dome shape. Then cut the cake in half *(fig 1)*.

2 Cover the two parts of the cake on separate cake boards or clean work surfaces.

3 Beginning with the base section of the cake spread buttercream over the top and sides using a palette knife.

4 Roll 300 g (11 oz) of the orangey-brown sugarpaste into a flat strip about 3 mm (⅛ in) thick. Cut out a rectangle approximately 50 cm (20 in) long and just a bit wider than the depth of the cake.
Roll the strip up like a bandage and unroll around the sides of the cake *(fig 2)*.

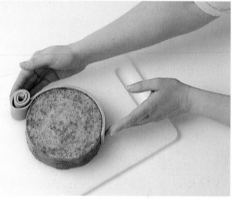

fig 2

Smooth the sides using smoothers and trim away any excess.

5 To make the lettuce, take the green sugarpaste and roll it out into a fairly thin strip. Place the strip on top of a piece of tin (aluminium) foil that has been crumpled and partially smoothed out *(fig 3)*. Run a rolling pin lightly over the sugarpaste on the tin foil and carefully peel the foil off. Cut it into strips and place around the edge of the bun allowing bits to overhang in a casual, lettucey sort of way.

6 For the burger, roll the dark brown sugarpaste into a thick circle about 15 cm (6 ¼ in) in diameter. Place this on top of the lettuce and then add texture to the burger by poking it with a drinking straw, No 3 nozzle (round tip) and the end of a paintbrush.

7 For the tomatoes, roll out the red sugarpaste and cut out six circles about 5.5 cm (2 ¼ in) in diameter. Press a line just inside each circle using either a circle cutter or the back of a knife. Then cut each circle in half *(fig 3)*. Make three lines across each segment with the back of a knife and finish off with a few pips made by pressing the tip of a No 3 piping nozzle into the tomato a few times.

8 Cover the top section of the cake with buttercream.

9 Roll out the remaining orangey-brown sugarpaste to a thickness of about 1 cm (¾ in). Although this is a bit thicker than you would usually use to cover a cake, it makes it much easier to get a smooth rounded finish so don't over do the

rolling out. Smooth the sides with smoothers and cut away any excess. Place the top in position on the tomatoes.

fig 3

10 Make tiny oval balls out of the orange sugarpaste and stick onto the top of the burger to look like sesame seeds. Keep the rest of the orange sugarpaste to use later.

11 Roll out the yellow sugarpaste to a thickness of about 3 mm (⅛ in) and cut out a square about 25 cm (10 in) square.

12 Moisten the cake board and lay the yellow sugarpaste on it in a crumpled manner.

13 Pick up the cake using a fish slice (pancake turner) and transfer it to the board.

14 Cut 10 g (¼ oz) of orange sugarpaste up into small strips and stick onto the yellow to look like French fries.

TIP: *If you want to adapt it to a cheeseburger, simply roll out 100 g (4 oz) yellow icing and cut out a square. Place it on top of the burger so that the corners are visible just below the tomatoes.*

TOADSTOOL

A lovely bold cake that should appeal to any child who believes in fairies and even those who don't. By covering the board, roof, window ledges and steps in white icing, this cake could easily be adapted into a magical snow-covered Christmas cake. The snail could have a Santa hat too.

INGREDIENTS

2 x 15 cm (6 in) round cakes
20 cm (8 in) round cake
3 quantities buttercream (see page 10)
1 kg (2 lb 4 oz) white sugarpaste (rolled fondant icing)
750 g (1 lb 10 oz) red sugarpaste (rolled fondant icing)
50 g (2 oz) brown sugarpaste (rolled fondant icing)
150 g (5 oz) black sugarpaste (rolled fondant icing)
75 g (3 oz) green sugarpaste (rolled fondant icing)
10 g (¼ oz) yellow sugarpaste (rolled fondant icing)
100 g (4 oz/½ cup) caster (superfine) sugar
Green and blue food colours
2 tbsp royal icing (see page 10)
icing (confectioners') sugar, for rolling out
Water

UTENSILS

30 cm (12 in) round cake board
20 cm (8 in) thin cake board
Carving knife
Small sharp knife
Palette knife (metal spatula)
Rolling pin
Cake smoothers
3 dowel rods (available from cake decorating shops)
Small hacksaw
Paintbrush
Circle cutters (optional)
Small bowl
Cocktail stick (toothpick), optional

1 Carve the 20 cm (8 in) cake into a rounded dome shape.

2 Now place the two smaller cakes on top of each other and carve into a slightly rounded base shape. Cut a thin strip off the top to ensure that the top is flat (*fig 1*).

fig 1

3 Place the stacked base cakes slightly towards the rear of the larger cake board. Slice the cakes and fill with buttercream. Reassemble the cakes and spread buttercream around the top and sides.

4 Knead and roll out 750 g (1 lb 10 oz) of white sugarpaste (rolled fondant icing) and use this to cover the base cakes. Lay the icing over the top of the two stacked base cakes and press it round. Neaten the sides with smoothers and trim away and keep any excess icing.

5 Spread a little buttercream onto the thin 20 cm (8 in) cake board and then place the round cake on top of it. Slice and fill the centre with buttercream and spread it over the top and sides. Roll out and cover the roof with the red sugarpaste. Smooth the icing and trim away any excess. Place the cake to one side for the moment.

6 Take the brown sugarpaste and partially knead a small ball of white icing into it to make a slight wood grain effect. Roll it out to a 3 mm (⅛ in) thickness and cut out an arched shape for the door. Stick this onto the front of the cake with a little water. Press the back of a knife vertically into the icing four times to leave the impression of wooden slats.

7 Roll out 50 g (2 oz) black sugarpaste to a 3 mm (⅛ in) thickness and cut out two smaller arch shapes for the windows. Stick one either side of the door with a little water.

8 Roll out 20 g (¾ oz) of white sugarpaste and cut four thin strips for the window frames about 5 mm (¼ in) wide. Stick two onto each window in the shape of a cross. Trim to fit.

9 Partially knead 275 g (10 oz) white sugarpaste together with 50 g (2 oz) of black to make a marbled stone

effect. Make about seven misshapen balls of differing sizes for the pebbles and two flattened ovals for the path. Put to one side. Make two window ledges, two steps for the front door and a frame that sits around the edge of the window (*fig 2*). Keep a small amount of the grey sugarpaste to make the door hinges (see step 11). Stick the steps, ledges and frames into place.

fig 2

10 Knead and thinly roll out the green sugarpaste. Cut this into pointed strips of different lengths and stick these around the side of the house.

11 Finish off the door with a tiny yellow door knocker. This is made out of a small ring of yellow sugarpaste topped with a tiny flattened yellow ball.

The hinges are made out of two tiny strips of grey sugarpaste, one straight, the other one shaped into a small 'W' shape and placed on its side.

fig 3

17 Now make the snail by partially kneading a little blue food colour into 25 g (1 oz) of white sugarpaste. Then roll it into a sausage approximately 15 cm (6 in) long. Roll it up and add a head made out of 10 g (⅓ oz) black sugarpaste. Finally add its feelers made out of a tiny string of black sugarpaste bent into a small 'V' shape.

TIP: *If the chimney won't stay in place and keeps sliding off the cake, thread the sections onto a cocktail stick (toothpick) and insert into the cake. But please be careful to remove it when cutting if children are eating the cake.*

12 Stick the three dowel rods into the base of the cake *(fig 3)* so that they rest on the cake board beneath. Make a small mark at the point at which they become level with the top of the cake. Pull them out and using a small hacksaw, trim them to size. Re-insert the rods back into the cake.

13 Smear about two tablespoons of royal icing over the top of the base cake and place the red roof cake into position. It's at this point that you find out why it is important to make the top of the base cakes as level as possible, otherwise the roof slides off while it's drying.

14 Make a small chimney out of 20 g (¾ oz) black sugarpaste. Roll half into a rounded shape with straight ends and the other half into a pointed triangular shape. Stick these onto the roof with a little water.

15 Thinly roll out 50 g (2 oz) of white sugarpaste. Using either circle cutters or the tip of a sharp knife, cut out about twelve spots of differing sizes. Stick these onto the roof with a little water.

16 For the grass, place the sugar into a small bowl and mix in a little green food colour.

Moisten the exposed cake board with a little water. Spoon the 'grass' over the board and position the pebbles and paving stones. Push the sugar into any awkward bits with a dry paintbrush.

HORRIBLE CHILD

If your child has a tendency towards cheekiness and you want to get your own back, this cake could well be the answer. Personalise it with your child's hair colour, perhaps making it longer if it's to be for a girl. You could also change the blue and white sweater to the colour of their favourite garment.

INGREDIENTS

20 cm (8 in) round cake
2 quantities buttercream
(see page 10)
950 g (1 lb 15 oz) flesh-
coloured sugarpaste
(rolled fondant icing)
215 g (7 ½ oz) white sugarpaste
(rolled fondant icing)
25 g (1 oz) black sugarpaste
(rolled fondant icing)
50 g (2 oz) brown sugarpaste
(rolled fondant icing)
25 g (1 oz) red sugarpaste
(rolled fondant icing)
50 g (2 oz) blue sugarpaste
(rolled fondant icing)
Icing (confectioners') sugar,
for rolling out
Water

UTENSILS

25 cm (10 in) round cake
board
Carving knife
Palette knife (metal spatula)
Small sharp knife
Rolling pin
Cake smoothers
4 cm (1 ¾ in) round cutter or
equivalent
2.5 cm (1 in) round cutter or
equivalent
Templates (see page 92)
Wooden spoon

fig 1

1 Level the top of the cake if necessary and turn the cake upside down. Slice and fill the centre with buttercream. Place the cake onto the cake board. Spread buttercream around the top and sides of the cake.

2 Roll out 800 g (1 lb 2 oz) of the flesh-coloured sugarpaste (rolled fondant icing) on a surface dusted with icing (confectioners') sugar. Cover the cake and smooth over the top and sides with your hands. Repeat using a pair of cake smoothers and trim away any excess from the base of the cake.

3 Thinly roll out 10 g (¼ oz) white sugarpaste. Cut out two 4 cm (1 ½ in) circles for the eyes. Stick onto the face with a little water. Roll out 10 g (¼ oz) black sugarpaste and cut out two 2.5 cm (1 in) circles. Stick these onto the white ones. Then stick a small flattened ball of white onto each eye to make a highlight.

4 Thinly roll out the brown sugarpaste. Place the hair template on top and cut around the edges with a scalpel. Lightly moisten the forehead with a little water and place the hair into position (*fig 1*).

5 Make a nose by rolling 50 g (1 ½ oz) of flesh-coloured sugarpaste into a ball. Stick this under the eyes.

6 To make the ears, cut a 4 cm (1 ½ in) circle out of a flat piece of flesh-coloured sugarpaste. Cut the circle in half and press the end of a wooden spoon into both ears to make an oval indent. Draw a small line around the dent

fig 2

using the tip of a sharp knife. Stretch both ears slightly and stick these into position with a little water.

7 Make a mouth out of a small flattened circle of black. Mould a tongue out of the red sugarpaste and stick into position (*fig 2*).

8 To make the hands, thinly roll out 100 g (4 oz) flesh-coloured sugarpaste. Position the hand template on top and cut around it. Repeat for the other hand (*see TIP*). Stick in place, lining up the edge of the wrists with the edge of the cake. Trim if necessary.

9 Roll out the remaining white sugarpaste into a thick sausage (rope) shape about 26 cm (10 in) long. Now moisten the cake board and lay the icing at the front of the cake (*fig 3*).

10 Thinly roll out the blue sugarpaste. Cut out two stripes 25 cm x 1 cm (10 in x ½ in). Stick these onto the white using water.

fig 3

TIP: *When cutting out the hands, turn the template over before starting the second one. Otherwise you'll end up with two right (or left) hands.*

DINOSAUR

Dinosaurs can sometimes be a problem because their legs are often fairly spindly in relation to their bodies. This cake gets round that by using the rock as a support. Although technically thousands of years separated the first man from the last dinosaur, I don't think you'll find many children complaining!

INGREDIENTS

23 cm (9 in) round cake
2 quantities buttercream (see page 10)
710 g (1 lb 6 ¼ oz) white sugarpaste (rolled fondant icing)
50 g (2 oz) black sugarpaste (rolled fondant icing)
525 g (1 lb 3 oz) green sugarpaste (rolled fondant icing)
25 g (1 oz) orange sugarpaste (rolled fondant icing)
50 g (2 oz) flesh-coloured sugarpaste (rolled fondant icing)
25 g (1 oz) dark green sugarpaste (rolled fondant icing)
Green, brown and black food colours
Dessicated (shredded) coconut

UTENSILS

30 cm (12 in) round cake board
Carving knife
Small sharp knife
Palette knife (metal spatula)
Rolling pin
Cake smoothers
Drinking straw
Paintbrushes, one medium, one fine
Small bowls x 2
Sieve (strainer)

fig 1

1 Cut and shape the cake into a misshapen rock shape (*fig 1*). (Use the pieces that you cut away from the sides to build up the height of the cake once it is on the cake board.)

2 Slice the cake and fill the centre with buttercream. Place it onto the cake board. Continue to spread the buttercream over the top and sides of the rock.

3 Take 700 g (1 lb 6 oz) white sugarpaste (rolled fondant icing) and the black sugarpaste and partially knead the two together to achieve a marbled effect.

4 Roll out the marbled grey sugarpaste. Place it over the cake. Smooth the sides with your hands and finish with cake smoothers. Trim away and keep the excess. Roll these bits into small round pebble shapes and put to one side for use later.

5 Make the dinosaur's back leg by rolling a 20 g (¾ oz) ball of green sugarpaste into a sausage (rope) about 10 cm (4 in) long (*fig 2*). Bend this into an 'L' shape and then make another bend at the end

of the foot for the toes. Making sure that the foot section rests on the ground, stick the leg against the rock using a little water.

6 Make the body using 450 g (1 lb) green sugarpaste. Knead and roll out the icing into a thick sausage about 20 cm (8 in) long. Continue to roll one end into a tapering tail and shape the other end into a head and neck.

7 Flatten the dinosaur slightly. (It should now measure about 44 cm (18 cm) from the end of tail to the tip of nose.) Then moisten the rock with a little water and wrap the dinosaur around it, by allowing the body to fall over the already positioned back leg.

8 Make a second back leg using 50 g (2 oz) green sugarpaste.

9 Make an arm by rolling 5 g (⅛ oz) of green sugarpaste into a sausage about 5 cm (2 in) long. Flatten one end and make three small cuts for fingers. Splay the fingers slightly and stick onto the body.

10 Stick a small almond shape of white sugarpaste onto the head to make an eye. Add a black circle and a small white flattened ball for a highlight. Finish the eye off with a thin green string of icing for an eyebrow.

11 Give the dinosaur scales by pressing a drinking straw held at a slight angle into the still soft icing and press the end of a paintbrush into the nose to make a nostril.

12 Stick little triangles of white sugarpaste along the edge of the mouth for teeth. The more teeth the better.

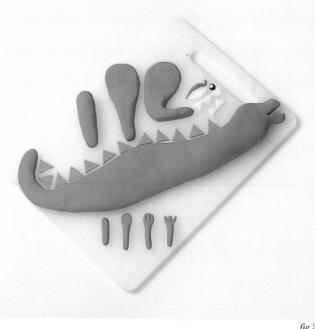

fig 2

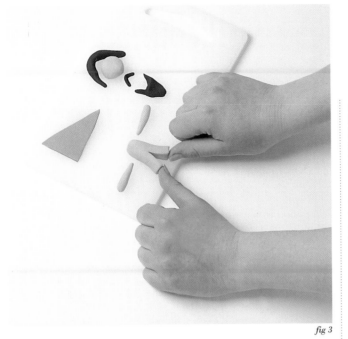

fig 3

13 Roll out 20 g (¾ oz) of orange surgarpaste and cut out 16 small triangles. Stick these along the dinosaur's back with a little water.

14 To make the little man (*fig 3*), roll 15 g (½ oz) flesh-coloured icing into a slightly tapered sausage shape. Make a cut from the wider end to about half way up and pull the icing apart slightly to make the legs. Bend the ends to make feet. Add a small ball for the head.

15 Place the man against the rock using a small amount of water to adhere him. Cut out a small, flat orange triangle and wrap this around his body.

16 Add two tiny arms, a beard and hair. Paint black splodges on his leopard skin and features on the face with black food colour.

17 Place some of the dessicated (shredded) coconut into a small bowl and mix with the green food colour. Repeat using more coconut and brown food colour in a separate bowl. Moisten the cake board and sprinkle the coloured dessicated coconut around the board. Place the extra rocks that were made earlier in place.

18 To make the greenery on the rock, push the green sugarpaste through a sieve (strainer). Slice it off with a knife, moisten the rock and stick it into position over the top and side.

TIP: *If making the man looks too difficult, substitute a jelly animal or even a plastic model or doll instead.*

U.F.O.

Most children (and a lot of the adults I know) have a fascination with the unexplained mysteries of the ether. So an unidentified flying cake landing on the tea table should cause a lot of interest. If it's for someone's birthday, insert birthday candles into the monster's tentacles and then turn down the lights for the full eerie effect.

INGREDIENTS

20 cm (8 in) round cake
1 quantity buttercream
(see page 10)
750 g (1 lb 10 oz) white
sugarpaste (rolled fondant
icing)
50 g (2 oz) black sugarpaste
(rolled fondant icing)
25 g (1 oz) yellow sugarpaste
(rolled fondant icing)
20 g (¾ oz) red sugarpaste
(rolled fondant icing)
40 g (1 ¾ oz) dark green
sugarpaste (rolled fondant
icing)
250 g (9 oz) dark blue
sugarpaste (rolled fondant
icing)
Small bit of liquorice (licorice)
bootlace
Water
Icing (confectioners') sugar,
for rolling out

UTENSILS

25 cm (10 in) square cake
board
Carving knife
Small sharp knife
Palette knife
Rolling pin
Cake smoothers
Small circle cutter
Paintbrush
Small plastic bags

fig 2

1 Slice about 2.5 cm (1 in) horizontally from the base of the cake. Turn this slice upside down and place it on the centre of the board. Carve and shape the remaining section of cake into a dome no bigger than 13 cm (5 in) diameter at the base. Place this in the middle of the first section of cake *(fig 1)*. Secure with a layer of buttercream.

fig 1

2 Cover the outside of the cake with buttercream.

3 Knead the white sugarpaste (rolled fondant icing) until pliable. Roll the icing out and cover the cake. Carefully smooth the sides and trim and keep any excess.

4 Knead the black sugarpaste and roll out thinly and using your icing nozzle or circle cutter, cut out about 50 circles. Roll out 10 g (¼ oz) of yellow sugarpaste and cut out about 8 circles.
Stick one line of black circles, interspersed occasionally by a yellow one (to look as though there's someone home!), around the base of the craft and another around the bottom of the top section *(fig 2)*.

5 Roll 10 g (½ oz) of red sugarpaste into a thin string and cut it up into about twenty-four 1 cm (½ in)

segments. Put one segment to one side (this will be used for the mouth and suckers later). Stick the rest of the segments around the middle of the cake, just below the top set of windows.

6 Make the monster's body out of 20 g (¾ oz) of green sugarpaste. Shape it into a small sausage (rope) first then slightly squeeze the icing about two thirds up to make a head. Sit the monster on the front of his craft *(fig 3)*. With the remaining green sugarpaste, make six legs (each about 6 cm/2 ½ in long) and six tiny flattened balls for suckers. Stick each leg into place and finish off with a sucker.

fig 3

7 Make yellow balls for eyes and stick into place. Add two tiny green eyeballs. Make a tiny ball of yellow for a nose. Add a red mouth and a small red ball to each sucker.

8 Insert two tiny strips of liquorice (licorice) into the monster's head and stick a little red ball of icing onto the

end of each one. Finish the monster off with a tiny yellow belly button.

9 Stick a small flattened 10 g (¼ oz) ball of blue sugarpaste onto the top of the spaceship. Then add a red and yellow ball. Score around the edge of the blue circle with the edge of a knife.

10 Moisten the exposed cake board with a little water.

11 Knead the dark blue sugarpaste and roll out thinly. Cover the board in sections (see page 12) and trim away the excess icing from the edges. Divide 10 g (¼ oz) of white sugarpaste into small balls. Flatten the balls slightly and stick around the board to look like planets.

TIP: *If you don't possess a small circle cutter, simply use an icing nozzle (tip) or something similar instead to make the windows.*

TEDDY CAKE

Not only would this make the ideal birthday cake for a first birthday but it could be used as a Christening cake too. If you are making it for a boy, simply substitute different hues of blue or yellow instead of the pink. Of course some adults are keen on teddies too – so don't restrict this cake to the children.

INGREDIENTS

15 cm (6 in) round cake
1 quantity buttercream (see page 10)
500 g (1 lb 2 oz) pale pink sugarpaste (rolled fondant icing)
375 g (13 oz) dark pink sugarpaste (rolled fondant icing)
100 g (3 oz) white sugarpaste (rolled fondant icing)
10 g (¼ oz) black sugarpaste (rolled fondant icing)
Black food colour
Water
Icing (confectioners') sugar, for rolling out

UTENSILS

20 cm (8 in) round cake board
Carving knife
Palette knife (metal spatula)
Small sharp knife
Rolling pin
Cake smoothers
Templates (see page 92)
Paintbrush

1 Slice off the top of the cake to level it if necessary and turn the cake upside down. Cut the cake in half.

2 Fill the centre with buttercream. Reassemble the cake and place it in the middle of the cake board. Spread buttercream around the sides and top using a palette knife (metal spatula).

3 Roll out the pale pink sugarpaste on a icing (confectioners') sugared surface to a thickness of about 1 cm (½ in). Lift and place over the cake. Smooth down the top and sides using your hands and a pair of cake smoothers. Trim and neaten the base.

4 Knead 75 g (3 oz) dark pink sugarpaste and roll out thinly. Using the templates, cut out a 10 cm (4 in) circle for the teddy's head, a 7.5 cm (3 in) semi-circle for the bear's body. Cut a 4 cm (1 ½ in) circle cut into two halves for the bear's ears. Re-knead the leftover icing and cut out the shape for the bear's arms. Cut this in two.

5 Stick the pieces onto the top of the cake and secure with water *(fig 1)*.

6 Roll out the white sugarpaste and cut out an oval about 7 cm (2 ¾ in) wide for the muzzle. Cut out two circles for the eyes and another for the centre of the ears. Slice this last one in half and stick one half onto each ear. Cut out three small curves and stick onto the bear's forehead.

7 Roll out the black sugarpaste and cut out two circles for the eyes. Cut a slightly larger one for the nose.

8 Stick a tiny flattened ball of white onto both the eyes and the nose.

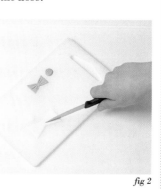
fig 2

9 Paint in the eyelashes and mouth using black food colour and a fine paintbrush.
  Make a small bow out of white sugarpaste *(fig 2)* and press the back of a knife into the icing a few times to make creases. Finish off with a small flattened ball of white icing. Stick onto the bear's chin. Make a smaller bow of dark pink sugarpaste and put aside.

10 Roll 150 g (5 oz) dark pink sugarpaste into strip 60 cm x 1 cm (24 in x ½ in). Moisten the top edge of the cake with a little water. Roll the sugarpaste up like a miniature bandage. Starting from the back of the cake, feed it out around the cake twisting the icing as you go *(fig 3)*. Roll the remaining dark pink sugarpaste into a strip 60 cm x 2 cm (24 in x ¾ in) and roll into a miniature bandage. Moisten the cake board with a little water and repeat the twisted effect around the base.

11 Finally hide the join at the top of the cake with the small dark pink bow you made earlier.

> **TIP:** *Trace and cut out the templates before you begin assembling the cake. It will make it quicker.*

fig 1

fig 3

SNAKE

A rare sighting of the tea time snake, Latin name 'Snakeus Cakeus'. He only ventures out once a year for birthdays and then tends to vanish quite quickly! You could substitute spots for the stripes if you prefer or even write the child's name along his back. Scatter a few sweet (candy) treats amongst the sand as well.

INGREDIENTS

Ingredients
23 cm (9 in) round sponge
2 quantities buttercream (see page 10)
1 kg (2 lb 4 oz) green sugarpaste (rolled fondant icing)
100 g (4 oz) red sugarpaste (rolled fondant icing)
100 g (4 oz) yellow sugarpaste (rolled fondant icing)
20 g (¾ oz) blue sugarpaste (rolled fondant icing)
250 g (9 oz) white sugarpaste (rolled fondant icing)
25 g (1 oz) black sugarpaste (rolled fondant icing)
175 g (6 oz/1¼ cups) soft brown sugar
Icing (confectioners') sugar, for rolling out
Water

UTENSILS

45 cm x 30 cm (18 in x 12 in) rectangular cake board
Carving knife
Small sharp knife
Palette knife (metal spatula)
Rolling pin
Cake smoothers
Paintbrush
Icing nozzle (tip) and drinking straw
About 30 jelly sweets (candies)
Small plastic bags

fig 2

fig 1

1 Shape the cake by first cutting it in half. Keeping the flat edges together, slide one semi-circle just over halfway along the other (*fig 1*). Cut another semi-circle out of each half so that the remaining cake forms an 'S' shape. Keep the two cut out centres. Round the edges of the snake. Carve the tail end into a point but leave the head end flat. Put the two small semi-circles of cake together to form a head and place this into position.

2 Slice the cake in half and fill the middle with buttercream. Spread buttercream along the sides and top as well.

3 Knead and roll out green sugarpaste (rolled fondant icing) into a strip about 60 cm (24 in) long. Wind the strip around a rolling pin. Lift it and unroll over the cake (*fig 2*). Ease the icing down over the sides and smooth with the cake smoothers. Trim away excess icing.

4 Knead the red and 100 g (4 oz) yellow sugarpaste and roll out thinly. Cut about eight strips out of both. (Keep the excess red for the tongue.)

5 Moisten the snake's back with a little water and lay the

strips over the cake, trimming them when necessary.

6 Add scales by holding an icing nozzle (tip) at a slight angle and pressing it into the still soft icing. Repeat with a drinking straw (*fig 3*).

7 Knead and roll the blue sugarpaste into a thin string and stick small sections onto the yellow stripes. Stick jelly sweets (candies) onto the snake's back. (They should stay in position with just a little water, but if your snake has a long way to slither to his party, it might be worth securing them with a little royal icing.)

8 Make two 50 g (2 oz) balls of white sugarpaste for eyes. Stick onto head.

9 Knead and roll out 10 g (¼ oz) black sugarpaste and cut out two black circles and a crescent for the eyes and mouth. Stick the circles onto the eyes and the mouth onto

the front of the face. Stick two tiny white circles onto the black eyes securing with a little water.

10 Cut a 'Y' shape out of red icing and stick onto the mouth with a little water.

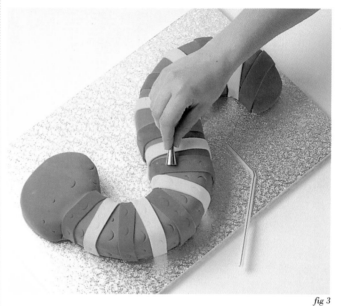

fig 3

11 Partially knead the remaining black sugarpaste into the remaining white sugarpaste. Pull off small sections and mould into pebbles.

12 Moisten the cake board and spoon the soft brown sugar over the board.

13 Place the pebbles into position.

TIP: *Don't panic if the icing cracks or creases slightly around the bends when you're covering the cake. Any slight blemishes can be covered by the stripes later.*

ENCHANTED HOUSE

You can make this cake as colourful as you like. Use whatever sweets (candies) take your fancy and if, after constructing the house, you find blemishes on the brickwork, use the sweets to hide them. If you can't get hold of 'hundreds and thousands' (rainbow nonpareils) for the path, use coloured sugar instead.

INGREDIENTS

2 x 15 cm (6 in) square sponges
2 quantities of buttercream (see page 10)
800 g (1 lb 12 oz) pink sugarpaste (rolled fondant icing)
50 g (2 oz) black sugarpaste (rolled fondant icing)
200 g (7 oz) white sugarpaste (rolled fondant icing)
50 g (2 oz) brown sugarpaste (rolled fondant icing)
10 g (¼ oz) grey sugarpaste (rolled fondant icing)
500 g (1 lb 2 oz) green sugarpaste (rolled fondant icing)
31 plain finger biscuits (cookies) (but have spares in case of breakages)
3 chocolate cream biscuits (cookies)
2 tbsp white royal icing (see page 10)
Edible gold balls
Assorted sweets, lollipops, candy canes
3 tsp 'hundreds and thousands' (rainbow nonpareils)
Water
Icing (confectioners') sugar, for rolling out on

UTENSILS

Utensils
30 cm (12 in) round cake board
Carving knife
Palette knife (metal spatula)
Rolling pin
Cake smoothers
Small sharp knife
Ruler
Piping (decorating) bag fitted with a No 3 nozzle (round tip)
Paintbrush

fig 1

1 Stack the two sponges on top of each other and cut the top one into a roof shape (*fig 1*). Slice the cakes and fill the layers with buttercream. Spread buttercream around the top and sides.

2 Knead the pink sugarpaste (rolled fondant icing) on a surface dusted with icing sugar until it's pliable. Roll it out and place it over the cake. Smooth the sides, first with your hands and then with a pair of cake smoothers. Trim away any excess.

3 Make the brickwork by holding a ruler horizontally and pressing it into the icing while it's still soft (*fig 2*). Press three lines into the sides of the house and six into the front and back. Press the back of a small knife vertically into the icing to pick out the individual bricks.

4 Split the chocolate cream biscuits in half to make the shutters. Roll the black icing out to a 3 mm (⅛ in) thickness. Measure the height of the biscuits (cookies) and make the height of the windows slightly shorter. Cut out three windows with a width of 2.5 cm (1 in) Stick the black icing windows into position with a little water. Roll out 10 g (¼ oz) white sugarpaste and cut out six strips. Place two on each window in the shape of a cross. Trim to fit and secure into position with a little

water. Using a little royal icing stick half a chocolate cream biscuit each side of each window to make the shutters.

5 Roll out the brown sugarpaste and cut out a rectangle 5 cm x 2.5 cm (2 in x 1 in). Stick this to the front of the house to make a door and holding a knife vertically, press the back of it into the icing to make the wooden slats of the door.

6 Divide the grey sugarpaste into two slightly misshapen rectangles and stick these against the door, one on top of the other to make the steps.

7 For the roof, break 25 finger biscuits in half. Starting at the bottom of one slope, make a line of five half biscuits, securing them with dabs of royal icing. Now add another line of biscuits above these and repeat a further three times. Do this again on the other side (*fig 3*). Lay five whole biscuits across the top of the roof.

8 Make a small chimney out of either a sweet (candy) or a small white and pink icing

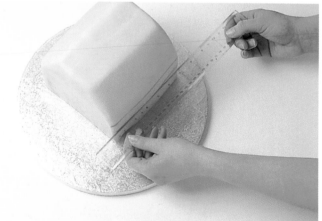

fig 2

fig 3

'sandwich' and position with royal icing. Stick a line of pink sweets along the top of the roof to decorate.

9 Decorate the shutters with sweets securing them with a little royal icing.

10 Pipe a line of royal icing above the door and press a finger biscuit into this to make the porch. Stick an edible gold ball in place for a door handle.

11 Pipe dots along the top and bottom of the windows.

12 Stick two 65 g (2 ½ oz) and one 50 g (2 oz) lumps of white sugarpaste onto the cake board with a little water.

13 Knead and roll out the green sugarpaste. Moisten the white 'lumps' and the exposed cake board. Lay the green around the house in sections (see page 11). Trim the edges of the board and cut and lift away a section at the front of the house to make a path.

14 Moisten the path with a little water and sprinkle with 'hundreds and thousands'

(rainbow nonpareils). Edge the sides of the path with small sweets inserted into the icing. Stick a few sweets to the side of the house and around the garden and secure with royal icing if necessary. Insert a couple of candy canes and lollipops into the green lumps.

TIP: *Score a thin line across the middle of each finger biscuit with a sharp knife before breaking them in half.*

PONY CAKE

A bright, bold eye-catching cake for horse-mad kids of all ages. If the young rider in question is lucky enough to own their own pony, give the icing horse similar markings. If you can get hold of any competition rosettes, these can be positioned around the cake board for an 'ambitious' finishing touch.

INGREDIENTS

15 cm (6 in) round cake
1 quantity buttercream (see page 10)
600 g (1 lb 6 oz) mid-green sugarpaste (rolled fondant icing)
65 g (2 ½ oz) light brown sugarpaste (rolled fondant icing)
25 g (1 oz) dark brown sugarpaste (rolled fondant icing)
20 g (¾ oz) white sugarpaste (rolled fondant icing)
10 g (¼ oz) black sugarpaste (rolled fondant icing)
25 g (1 oz) biscuit yellow sugarpaste (rolled fondant icing)
150 g (5 oz) orange sugarpaste (rolled fondant icing)
25 g (1 oz) dark green sugarpaste (rolled fondant icing)
Icing (confectioners') sugar, for rolling out
Water

UTENSILS

20 cm (8 in) round cake board
Carving knife
Small sharp knife
Palette knife (metal spatula)
Rolling pin
Cake smoothers
Templates (see page 93)
Scalpel
Paintbrush
Small plastic bags

1 Slice off the top of the cake to level it if necessary and turn it upside down on the cake board. Slice the cake and fill the middle with buttercream. Spread a layer of buttercream over the top and sides as well.

2 Knead and roll out 500 g (1 lb 2 oz) of the mid-green sugarpaste (rolled fondant icing) and cover the cake. Smooth the top and sides and trim away any excess icing and put this with the remainder of the mid-green icing.

3 Roll out the light brown sugarpaste to a thickness of about 3 mm (⅛ in). Place the horse's head template onto the sugarpaste and trace around it with a scalpel or the tip of a sharp knife (fig 1). Moisten the top of the cake and place the head in position.

fig 1

4 Roll out the dark brown icing to a thickness of 1.5 mm (¹⁄₁₆ in) and cut out three small strips for the pony's bridle. Stick them into position with a little water and trim to fit.

5 Roll out about half of the white sugarpaste until it's

fig 2

about 3mm (⅛ in) thick and cut out a 3 cm (1¼ in) circle for the horse's eye. Stick this into position and then add a thin black circle about 2 cm (¾ in) Finally add a highlight made out of a tiny flattened ball of white sugarpaste. Cut a semi-circle the same diameter as the eye out of the light brown sugarpaste and place over the eye (fig 2).

6 To make the horse's bit, cut out a small white circle and stick it just to the side of the horse's mouth. Stick a smaller circle of black in the centre and place another flattened ball of black just above to form the horse's nostril. Add a thin string of black sugarpaste along the base of the horse's eyelid to make an eyelash.

7 Roll out the biscuit-yellow sugarpaste and cut out the mane using the template if necessary. Stick this onto the neck with a little water.

8 Add two ears made from light brown sugarpaste.

9 To cover the cake board, roll the remaining mid-green sugarpaste into a strip about

60 cm (24 in) long. Cut away one long edge and roll the icing up like a bandage (see page 11). Moisten the exposed cake board and starting at the back, unwind the strip around the base of the cake. Trim away the excess.

10 Divide the orange sugarpaste into about fifteen pieces. Roll each one into a tapering carrot shape and press about five lines into the top of each carrot with back of a knife (fig 3).

fig 3

11 Using the dark green sugarpaste, make a small green flattish triangle. Make three cuts and splay the three 'fingers'.

12 Make a small dent in the end of each carrot with the tip of a paintbrush and insert a carrot top. Repeat with the rest of the carrots and position them around the top and base of the cake.

TIP: *If stored in a box with a lid to keep the dust off, the carrots can be made up to a week before.*

COMPUTER GAME

The perfect cake with which to tempt junior away from his computer game for a while. If you don't feel competent about painting onto the screen, substitute a photograph or a picture cut out of a comic or magazine instead. Stick it onto a thin bit of cardboard and secure onto the cake with a little royal icing.

INGREDIENTS

18 cm (7 in) square cake
1 quantity buttercream (see page 10)
400 g (14 oz) black sugarpaste (rolled fondant icing)
800 g (1 lb 12 oz) blue sugarpaste (rolled fondant icing)
50 g (2 oz) grey sugarpaste (rolled fondant icing)
20 g (¾ oz) red sugarpaste (rolled fondant icing)
10 g (¼ oz) yellow sugarpaste (rolled fondant icing)
black food colour
Icing (confectioners') sugar, for rolling out
Water

UTENSILS

25 cm (10 in) square cake board
Carving knife
Small sharp knife
Palette knife (metal spatula)
Rolling pin
Cake smoothers
Fish slice (pancake turner)
Circle cutters or equivalent
Paintbrushes, one medium, one fine

1 Cover the cake board with 350 g (12 oz) black sugarpaste (rolled fondant icing) (see page 11). Put the board to one side.

fig 1

2 Cut about a third off one side of the cake. Place the cut off section against one of the shorter sides of the cake to increase the length of the cake (fig 1). Trim to fit.

3 Cut a small semi-circle out of one of the longer sides and place this against the opposite side of the cake (fig 2).

4 Run a sharp knife around the edges of the cake to make them rounded.

5 Slice the cake in half and fill the centre with buttercream. Spread buttercream over the top and sides with a palette knife (metal spatula).

6 Knead the blue sugarpaste until pliable. Roll it out and cover the cake. Smooth the sides with cake smoothers and trim away any excess.

7 Carefully lift the cake using a fish slice and place it diagonally on the black sugarpasted cake board.

8 Roll out the grey sugarpaste and cut out a rectangle for the screen 7.5 cm x 5 cm (3 in x 2 in). Stick this in the centre of the cake using a little water.

9 Using the back of a knife, indent five lines each side of the screen.

10 Thinly roll out the red sugarpaste and cut out two circles 4 cm (1 ½ in) in diameter. Stick one either side of the screen below the indented lines.

11 Paint the design onto the screen using black food colour and a fine paintbrush (fig 3).

12 Roll out the yellow sugarpaste and cut out a small cross and stick this onto one of the red circles. Stick a small yellow circle onto the other one. Cut out two yellow

fig 3

rectangles and one red one and stick these below the screen with a little water.

13 Roll 10 g (¼ oz) of black sugarpaste into a thin string and stick along the edge of the screen.

14 Roll the rest of the black sugarpaste into a slightly thicker string about 28 cm (11 in) long and lay this along the bottom edge of the game.

15 Roll out the rest of the blue sugarpaste and cut out about 16 circles. Use these to decorate the board.

TIP: *Add the ultimate psychedelic touch to the inside too by swirling a bit of food colour into the cake mixture before baking.*

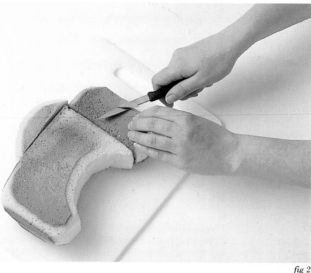

fig 2

RAG DOLL

A smiling, edible doll that should please any little girl. Dress the doll in the child's favourite colours – or you could even copy her favourite dress if you're feeling particularly enterprising. If you find the sugar flowers a bit fiddly, arrange sweets (candies) or small biscuits (cookies) around the board instead.

INGREDIENTS

15 cm (6 in) round cake
15 cm (6 in) square cake
2 quantities of buttercream
(see page 10)
500 g (1 lb 2 oz) pale pink sugarpaste (rolled fondant icing)
450 g (1 lb) flesh-coloured sugarpaste (rolled fondant icing)
250 g (9 oz) white sugarpaste (rolled fondant icing)
500 g (1 lb 2 oz) yellow sugarpaste (rolled fondant icing)
350 g (12 oz) brown sugarpaste (rolled fondant icing)
20 g (¾ oz) dark pink sugarpaste (rolled fondant icing)
50 g (2 oz) black sugarpaste (rolled fondant icing)
Black and blue food colours
Icing (confectioners') sugar, for rolling out
Water

UTENSILS

30 cm x 40 cm (12 in x 16 in) rectangular cake board
Carving knife
Small sharp knife
Palette knife (metal spatula)
Rolling pin
Cake smoothers
Fish slice (pancake turner)
No 3 piping nozzle (round tip)
Paintbrushes, one medium, one fine
Small plastic bags

1 Moisten the entire cake board with a little water and cover with the pale pink sugarpaste (see page 11). Trim away the excess and put the board to one side.

2 Cut the round cake into a rounded dome shape for the head. The diameter at the base should measure about 12.5 cm (5 in).

3 To make the doll's body, cut two triangles off the sides of the square cake to leave a shape that resembles a roof. Then cut a slope into the neck end (*fig 1*).

fig 1

4 Slice and fill the centres of both cakes with buttercream. Then cover the tops and sides of the cakes with buttercream.

5 Cover the head with 250 g (9 oz) flesh-coloured icing. Trim off any excess and smooth it. Lift it with a fish slice (pancake turner) into position on the board. Place the buttercreamed body into position beneath the head.

6 Add two legs, each made from a 100 g (4 oz) sausage (rope) of white sugarpaste. Stick to the board with a little water.

7 Knead and roll out the yellow sugarpaste. Cut out a sort of roof shape for the dress, 15 cm (6 in) wide at the

top, 30 cm (12 in) wide at the bottom and 23 cm (9 in) long. Drape it over the doll's body allowing it to fall onto the legs. Neaten the sides if necessary

8 Press the tip of a No 3 nozzle (round tip) along the base of the hem to produce a pattern (*fig 2*). Keep the excess yellow icing to one side.

9 Make two arms, each one made out of 100 g (4 oz) flesh-coloured icing. Flatten the hands slightly and make two partial cuts for fingers. Make another cut right through the icing for the thumb. Splay the thumb slightly. Place the arms into position using water.

10 To make the collar, roll out 50 g (2 oz) yellow icing and cut a strip 18 cm x 2.5 cm (7 in

x 1 in) long. Stick along the top of the dress. Press the tip of a No 3 nozzle along the base of the collar.

11 Roll out 200 g (7 oz) of brown icing and cut out two large almond shapes and stick one to each side of the head. Score four lines down each side of the hair with the back

fig 2

of a knife. Cut a triangle out of the excess and cut it to make a fringe (bangs).

12 Make a plait (braid) out of 50 g (2 oz) brown sugarpaste. Roll it into a sausage (rope) about 33 cm (13 in) long. Fold the sausage in half and twist the icing together (*fig 3*). Moisten the side of the head and board with water and stick into

position. Repeat on the other side. Add a small fringe to the end of each plait using about 10 g (¼ oz).

13 Make two small bows out of four small triangles and two flattened balls of dark pink icing. Position them on the the end of the plaits.

14 Cut out two flat circles about 2.5 cm (1 in) diameter of white sugarpaste for the eyes. Stick them into position. Add two smaller black circles and a flattened ball of white. Position a small ball of flesh-coloured icing for a nose. Paint the mouth and eyelashes with a fine paintbrush and black food colour.

15 Paint the stripes onto the legs with blue food colour.

16 Make flowers out of the remaining white and yellow sugarpaste. Using the No 3 piping nozzle as a cutter, cut out five white circles and one yellow per flower. Stick the five white circles in a ring and top with a yellow centre.

TIP: *Use the flowers to cover up any marks or blemishes on the board.*

fig 3

SOCCER

Colour the scarf in the recipient's favourite team's sporting colours and use it to hide any mistakes you might make when carving and covering the cake. If you really don't fancy the idea of shaping a rounded cake, it is possible to buy circular baking tins (pans) that do all the hard work for you.

INGREDIENTS

15 cm (6 in) round cake
1 quantity of buttercream (see page 10)
1 kg (2 lb 4 oz) white sugarpaste (rolled fondant icing)
50 g (2 oz) black sugarpaste (rolled fondant icing)
200 g (7 oz) blue (or the favoured team's colours) sugarpaste (rolled fondant icing)
50 g (2 oz) green coloured sugar (see page 10)
Icing (confectioners') sugar, for rolling out
Water

UTENSILS

23 cm (9 in) round cake board
Carving knife
Small sharp knife
Palette knife (metal spatula)
Rolling pin
Cake smoothers
Template for hexagon (see page 93)
Scalpel
Paintbrush
Teaspoons
Small plastic bags

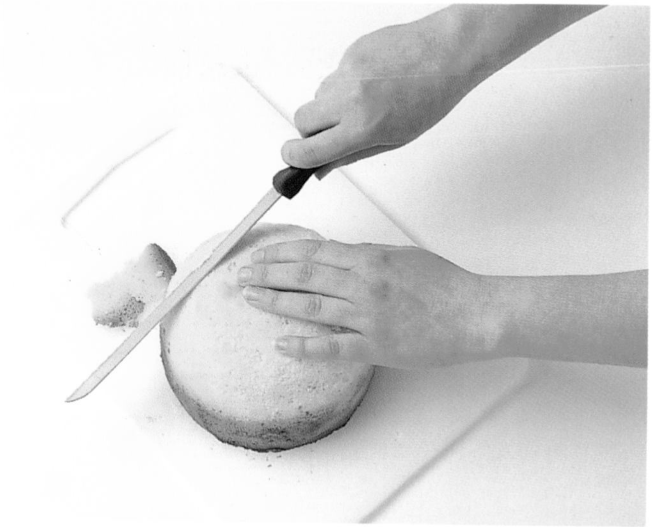

fig 1

1 Carve the cake into a rounded dome shape (fig 1).

2 Slice the cake in half and fill the centre with buttercream. Continue to spread the buttercream around the top and sides. Place the cake in the centre of the board.

3 Knead and roll out half of the white sugarpaste (rolled fondant icing) and cover the cake. Trim away and keep any excess from the base. Run over the surface with a cake smoother.

4 Roll out the black sugarpaste and 200 g (7 oz) of white. Using the template and a scalpel or sharp knife, cut out 20 white hexagons and seven black hexagons.

5 Starting with a black hexagon in the centre of the cake, surround it with a circle of white ones. Build up the pattern, securing the hexagons with water (fig 2). When all the hexagons are in place, run over the surface with a cake

smoother again to make them lie neat and flat.

6 Knead the remainder of the white sugarpaste until pliable. Roll it out and cut a strip about 50 cm x 7.5 cm (20 in x 3 in) to form the scarf.

7 Moisten the sides of the cake and wrap the scarf around (fig 3).

fig 3

8 Roll out the blue sugarpaste and cut into stripes. Stick these onto the scarf securing them with water. Roll out and cut a white rectangle into a fringe. Stick onto the end of the scarf.

9 Moisten the exposed cake board and spoon the coloured sugar around the scarf.

TIP: *When you have cut out the hexagons, place a sheet of clingfilm (plastic wrap) over the top of them to stop them drying out and cracking before you stick them on.*

fig 2

CAT AND MOUSE

Who says that mice are always scared of cats? This one certainly isn't! Make the markings on the cat similar to those of your own pet, or the intended recipient's, and save time on 'cake decorating day' by making the mouse a few days in advance or even substituting a shop-bought sugar one instead.

INGREDIENTS

18 cm (7 in) round cake
1½ quantities of buttercream (see page 10)
350 g (12 oz) red sugarpaste (rolled fondant icing)
1 kg (2 lb 4 oz) orangey-brown sugarpaste (rolled fondant icing)
10 g (¼ oz) green sugarpaste (rolled fondant icing)
20 g (¾ oz) pink sugarpaste (rolled fondant icing)
20 g (¾ oz) black sugarpaste (rolled fondant icing)
100 g (4 oz) dark brown sugarpaste (rolled fondant icing)
25 g (1 oz) grey sugarpaste (rolled fondant icing)
Liquorice (licorice) bootlace
Icing (confectioners') sugar, for rolling out
Water

UTENSILS

30 cm (12 in) round cake board
Carving knife
Small sharp knife
Palette knife (metal spatula)
Fish slice (pancake turner)
Rolling pin
Cake smoothers
Paintbrush
Cocktail stick (toothpick)

1 Cover the 30 cm (12 in) round cake board with the red sugarpaste (rolled fondant icing) (see page 11). Place this board to one side.

fig 1

2 On either a spare cake board or a clean work surface (counter top), cut the cake into an oval shape that tapers and slopes towards the front (*fig 1*). Slice and fill the centre with buttercream and continue to spread the buttercream carefully over the top and sides.

3 Roll out 500 g (1 lb 2 oz) of the orangey-brown sugarpaste to a 5 mm (¼ in) thickness. Lift and place over the cake. Smooth down the icing first with your hands, then with a pair of cake smoothers and trim away any excess.

4 Lift the cake using a fish slice (pancake turner). Slide the fish slice under the back and place the cake towards the rear of the sugarpasted board. Be careful not to damage the sugarpaste.

5 To make the head (*fig 2*), roll 300 g (11 oz) of the orangey-brown sugarpaste into a large flattish oval shape. Place into position and stick with a little water.

6 Cut two flat almond shapes out of the green sugarpaste and stick onto the face.

7 To make the ears, cut two small orangey-brown triangles and stick these onto the top of the head.
    Thinly roll out 10 g (¼ oz) pink sugarpaste and cut out two smaller triangles and stick these inside the ears. Bend the tips of the ears forward slightly.

8 Make the eyebrows by rolling 10 g (¼ oz) of black sugarpaste into a thin sausage (rope). Cut this in half and bend each half into an 'S' shape. Stick one above each eye.

9 Stick a small flattened black circle onto each eye and finish off with a tiny ball of white for a highlight.

10 Make a nose out of a small rounded pink triangle. Then make a flattened black circle for a mouth.

11 For the whiskers, cut a liquorice (licorice) bootlace into short lengths about 9 cm (3 ½ in) long. Insert these into the cat's face while the icing is still soft. (See TIP.)

fig 2

12 To make the cat's tail, roll 100 g (4 oz) of the orangey-brown sugarpaste into a thick sausage and stick this into position.

13 To make the stripes, thinly roll out the brown sugarpaste. Cut out four strips for the cat's back and about 10 small strips for the tail. Also cut out a triangle for the cat's head and stick this between the cat's ears.

14 To make the mouse, roll 20 g (¾ oz) of grey sugarpaste into a cone shape. Bend the top forward slightly to make a

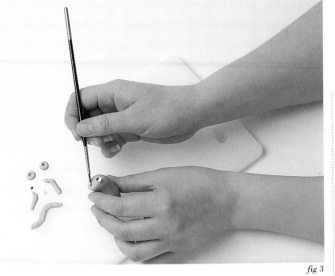
fig 3

head. Stick two tiny grey balls to the top of the head for ears and indent each ear with the end of a paintbrush. For the arms, make two small grey

strands. Flatten and bend the ends to form hands and stick one either side of the head. Secure with a little water if necessary.

15 Make two eyes out of two tiny white and two even tinier balls of black. Add a pink nose and a pink triangle for his sticking out tongue *(fig 3)*.

Make a small tail out of a thin pink sausage and stick behind the mouse's body. Indent the tail using the back of a knife.

TIP: *To prevent the icing from cracking when inserting the liquorice, first make a small hole using a cocktail stick (toothpick).*

DOPEY DOG

The way to give someone who wants a puppy for their birthday a dog – without all the chewed slippers and 'little presents' that usually accompany the real thing. This is the ideal cake and for both dog and cake lovers alike. If you're feeling adventurous, try and base the markings of the dog on the family pet or a favourite breed.

INGREDIENTS

18 cm (7 in) round cake
1 quantity buttercream
(see page 10)
600 g (1 lb 6 oz) brown
sugarpaste (rolled fondant
icing)
50 g (2 oz) flesh-coloured
sugarpaste (rolled fondant
icing)
165 g (5½oz) black sugarpaste
(rolled fondant icing)
25 g (1 oz) white sugarpaste
(rolled fondant icing)
150 g (5 oz) red sugarpaste
(rolled fondant icing)
About 12 edible silver
coloured balls
Icing (confectioners') sugar,
for rolling out
Water

UTENSILS

23 cm (9 in) round cake board
Small sharp knife
Carving knife
Palette knife (metal spatula)
Rolling pin
Template (see page 93)
Cake smoothers
Paintbrush
Small plastic bags

fig 1

1 Level the top of the cake if necessary and turn the cake upside down. Cut the shape of the dog's head out of the cake using the template (fig 1).

2 Slice the cake in half and fill the centre with buttercream. Spread buttercream over the top and sides and place the cake onto the board.

3 Roll out the brown sugarpaste (rolled fondant icing) and cover the cake with it. Neaten and flatten the sides using smoothers. Trim away and keep the excess.

4 Knead and roll out the flesh-coloured sugarpaste and cut out a large oval shape. Stick this onto the muzzle area with water and trim away any excess from the bottom (fig 2).

5 Make a 20 g (¾ oz) ball of black sugarpaste for the nose and stick into position with a little water.

6 Use 10 g (¼ oz) of black sugarpaste for the mouth. Roll the icing into a thin string approximately 10 cm (4 in) – the length will depend on the depth of your cake – and stick it onto the muzzle and down the side of the cake.

7 Mould 75 g (3 oz) of red sugarpaste into a tongue and stick this onto the mouth, with the thickest part resting on the brown sugarpaste beneath the eye.

8 Make three small flattened balls out of black sugarpaste and stick above the tongue.

9 Roll out 10 g (¼ oz) white sugarpaste and cut out an oval shape for the eye. Slice the base off the oval and stick this into position on the dog's head, securing with water.

10 Roll 10 g (¼ oz) black sugarpaste into a thin string and cut off a section about 13 cm (5 in) long. Now place this round the eye, trimming the ends if necessary so that they line up with the base of the eye.

11 Place another black sugarpaste 'string' about 6 cm (2 ½ in) long under the eye.

12 Add a black eyeball and finish with a flattened white ball of icing as a highlight.

13 Make an ear by cutting a leaf shape out of 40 g (1 ½ oz) black sugarpaste. Moisten the cake board above the dog's nose and ease the ear into position. Make another ear out of 65 g (2 ½ oz) black sugarpaste and stick this onto the top of the cake, bending the top of the ear slightly back on itself as you lay it down (fig 3).

Knead the remaining red sugarpaste until pliable and roll out. Cut a strip approximately 23 cm x 2.5 cm (9 in x 1 in) and place around the dog's neck. Press the silver balls into the collar and secure with a little water.

Make a couple of dog biscuits by kneading a little brown icing into 20 g (¾ oz) white sugarpaste. Divide into two slightly flattened balls and poke six holes into the top of each biscuit with the end of a paintbrush. Stick onto the board with water (fig 3).

fig 3

TIP: *If the silver balls refuse to stay put, stick them with a little red-coloured royal icing.*

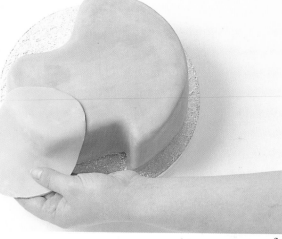

fig 2

STUFFED ELEPHANT

Now here's a real party animal! Although this cake appears in the children's section, I rather suspect he will appeal to many adults as well as we have all felt how he looks at some time or another. If you wanted to dress him up a bit, you could attach a bow around his neck or place a few party streamers around the board.

INGREDIENTS

15 cm (6 in) round cake
1 quantity buttercream (see page 10)
350 (12 oz) pale blue sugarpaste (rolled fondant icing)
1.15 kg (2 lb 5 oz) pale pink sugarpaste (rolled fondant icing)
50 g (2 oz) white sugarpaste (rolled fondant icing)
20 g (¾ oz) black sugarpaste (rolled fondant icing)
10 g (¼ oz) dark pink sugarpaste (rolled fondant icing)
1 tbsp dark pink royal icing (see page 10)
Icing (confectioners') sugar, for rolling out
Water

UTENSILS

30 cm (12 in) round cake board
Carving knife
Small sharp knife
Palette knife (metal spatula)
Rolling pin
Cake smoothers
Wooden spoon
Fish slice (pancake turner)
Piping bag fitted with No 2 (round tip) nozzle
Paintbrush
Clingfilm (plastic wrap)

1 Lightly moisten the cake board with a little water. Roll out the pale blue sugarpaste (rolled fondant icing) and use this to cover the board (see page 11). Trim and neaten the edges and place the board to one side.

fig 1

2 Carve the cake into a rounded shape on a spare cake board or clean work surface (countertop). Slice it in half and fill the centre with buttercream. Spread buttercream around the sides and top as well and cover the cake using 500 g (1 lb 2 oz) of pale pink sugarpaste. Smooth and trim away any excess and lift the cake and place it towards the rear of the covered cake board using a fish slice (pancake turner). Be careful not to get any indents or fingerprints on the sugarpaste (*fig 1*).

3 Make a head using 300 g (11 oz) of pale pink icing. Mould it into a chunky tennis racquet sort of shape. Flatten the head slightly and pinch around the edge of the trunk to make a slight rim. Moisten the body and cake board and place the head into position. Press the end of a wooden spoon into the end of the trunk to make the nostrils and use the back of a knife to make a few creases across the top of the trunk.

4 Make four pink 50 g (2 oz) chunky carrot shapes for the legs and stick into position. Cut out four 2.5 cm (1 in) white circles and stick one to the pad of each foot.

5 Make two 50 g (2 oz) pale pink ovals for the ears and stick one either side of the head using a couple of scrunched up balls of clingfilm (plastic wrap) to support the backs of the ears whilst they are drying (*fig 2*). Cut out two smaller white ovals and stick these inside the ears.

6 Make a thin, tapering sausage (rope) shape for the tail out of 20 g (¾ oz) of pale pink sugarpaste.

7 For the eyes, cut out two 2.5 cm (1 in) round circles of white sugarpaste and stick these in place. Add two 2 cm (¾ in) black circles and finish with two tiny flattened balls of white as highlights.

8 Add two thin black sausage shapes as eyebrows and a fringe (bangs) cut out of the dark pink sugarpaste.

9 Put the pink royal icing into a piping (decorating) bag fitted with a No 2 piping nozzle (round tip) and and pipe dots onto the board (*fig 3*).

fig 3

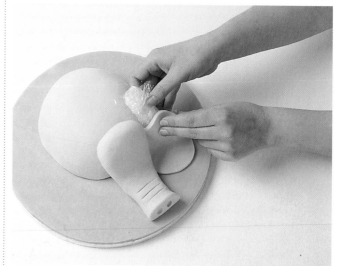

fig 2

TIP: *If you feel that the piping all those spots would make you go 'dotty', substitute sweets (candies) instead.*

ADULTS' CAKES

Many of the cakes in this section have been designed to tie in with favourite pastimes, so amongst the ideas here you will find cakes for avid golfers, motor racing fans and shopaholics, plus a yacht for those who dream of sailing away from the creative mess in the kitchen!

FISHERMAN

Fishing is apparently one of the most popular hobbies so there must be hundreds of wet and bedraggled fishermen sitting out there in the wind and the rain who would appreciate a cake like this when they get home. If it's the fisherman's birthday, the rocks double up as ideal candle holders.

INGREDIENTS

15 cm (6 in) round cake
1 quantity buttercream (see page 10)
550 g (1 lb 4 oz) brown sugarpaste (rolled fondant icing)
50 g (2 oz) black sugarpaste (rolled fondant icing)
40 g (1½ oz) flesh-coloured sugarpaste (rolled fondant icing)
185 g (6 oz) dark green sugarpaste (rolled fondant icing)
100 g (4 oz) white sugarpaste (rolled fondant icing)
50 g (2 oz) green sugarpaste (rolled fondant icing)
3 tbsp royal icing, (see page 10)
Green and blue food colours
Water
Icing (confectioners') sugar, for rolling out

UTENSILS

25 cm (10 in) round cake board
Carving knife
Small sharp knife
Palette knife (metal spatula)
Rolling pin
Cake smoothers
Cocktail stick (toothpick)
No 3 piping nozzle (round tip)
Sieve (strainer)
Small bowl
8 jelly (candy) fish
Needle and thread
Black boot cut out of a small piece of thin cardboard
Wooden skewer, trimmed to about 20 cm (8 in)

1 Carve the cake into shape (*fig 1*). Cut slopes into the sides and then cut a small semi-circle out of the side of the cake to make a bit of an inlet. Place the cut-out bits on top of the cake to make a hill.

fig 1

2 Place the cake onto the board. Slice it in half, fill and cover with buttercream.

3 Roll out 500 g (1 lb 2 oz) of brown sugarpaste (rolled fondant icing) to a thickness of about 1 cm (½ in). Lift and cover the cake. Smooth the sides. Trim and keep the excess.

4 To make the fisherman's body, knead the remaining brown sugarpaste into a ball. Place it in position on the cake and secure with a little water.

5 To make the legs, take two 20 g (¾ oz) lumps of black sugarpaste and roll each one into a sausage (rope) about 7.5 cm (3 in) long. Bend the end of each leg into an 'L' shape to make the feet. Stick the legs into position. Insert a cocktail stick into the top of the body, leaving about 1 cm (½ in) protruding.

6 Roll 25 g (1 oz) flesh-coloured sugarpaste into a ball for the head. Moisten the neck and thread onto the stick.

7 Roll out 150 g (5 oz) dark green sugarpaste to a thick-

fig 2

ness of about 3 mm (⅛ in). Cut out a strip approximately 23 cm x 7.5 cm (9 in x 3 in). Moisten the body and wrap it round (*fig 2*). Press the tip of a No 3 piping nozzle (round tip) into the sugarpaste to make a line of buttons up the front of the coat. Make two sausages out of 10 g (¼ oz) of green sugarpaste for the arms. Stick into place. Add two small ovals of flesh-coloured sugarpaste for hands and

another ball for a nose and a strip of brown sugarpaste for the hair. Moisten the top of the head and stick a small flat 5 cm (2 in) circle onto it for a hat. Bend the front up slightly to make a peak.

8 Partially knead the remaining black sugarpaste into 50 g (2 oz) white. Mould the marbled sugarpaste into odd-sized balls for rocks.

9 Moisten the area of land behind the fisherman. Knead the green sugarpaste until pliable then push bits through a sieve (strainer). Cut off the strands and place into position.

10 Put 3 tbsp royal icing into a bowl and partially mix in a little green and blue food colours. Swirl the coloured icing around the cake board using a small palette knife (metal spatula) and place the rocks and jelly (candy) fish into position (*fig 3*). Wipe round the edge of the board with a damp cloth.

11 Using a needle, thread the cotton through the top of the cardboard wellington boot and tie a knot. Tie the other end to the wooden skewer.

fig 3

12 Carefully insert the wooden skewer through the fisherman's lap and make sure that the wellington boot is positioned properly.

TIP: *A few strands of spaghetti can be used instead of a cocktail stick, inside the fisherman's body if preferred.*

HANDYMAN

The ideal cake for anyone to who likes to wield a hammer or the perfect hint for someone you wish would! Give the sponge itself a 'wood' effect by partially mixing a couple of teaspoons of cocoa into the madeira mixture before it's cooked. Once baked, it should have an interesting marbled look to it.

INGREDIENTS

15 cm (6 in) square cake
1 quantity buttercream (see page 10)
60 g (2¼ oz) orange gelatin icing (see page 10)
50 g (2 oz) grey gelatin icing (see page 10)
600 g (1 lb 6 oz) white sugarpaste (rolled fondant icing)
20 g (¾ oz) grey sugarpaste (rolled fondant icing)
50 g (2 oz) red sugarpaste (rolled fondant icing)
50 g (2 oz) black sugarpaste (rolled fondant icing)
50 g (2 oz) tan sugarpaste (rolled fondant icing)
10 g (¼ oz) blue sugarpaste (rolled fondant icing)
20 g (¾ oz) orange sugarpaste (rolled fondant icing)
Royal icing, (optional, see page 10)
Cornflour (cornstarch)
Dark brown, chestnut and black food colours
Icing (confectioners') sugar, for rolling out
Water

UTENSILS

20 cm (8 in) square cake board
Templates for saw (page 93)
Scalpel
Spare cake board
Rolling pin
Carving knife
Sharp knife
Palette knife (metal spatula)
Cake smoothers
Paintbrushes, one medium, one fine

1 Roll out the grey gelatin icing to a thickness of 3 mm (⅛ in). Place the saw template onto the icing and cut out the shape using a scalpel. (Although a sharp knife will do the job adequately, it's a lot easier with a scalpel.)

2 Roll out the orange gelatin icing and, using the templates, cut out two handle shapes. Place the three gelatin icing pieces onto a spare cake board that has been lightly dusted with cornflour (cornstarch) and leave to dry overnight.

3 Slice the top off the cake to level it and turn it upside down. Cut the cake in half and fill the centre with buttercream. Spread more buttercream around the sides and over the top.

4 Place the cake slightly off centre on the cake board so that there is a wider expanse of cake board showing at the front and on the right-hand side.

5 Put 20 g (¾ oz) of the white sugarpaste (rolled fondant icing) to one side. Carefully roll the dark brown and chestnut food colours into the icing to achieve a nice wood-grain effect (see page 10). Roll out the icing and cover the cake and smooth the sides. Trim away and keep the excess. Finish neatening the sides with a pair of cake smoothers.

6 Cut a thin strip out of the cake, ready for the saw, while the icing is still soft. Make a 5 mm (¼ in) wide cut from the base of the cake to about halfway across the top of the cake. Lift this section of cake out and discard (fig 1).

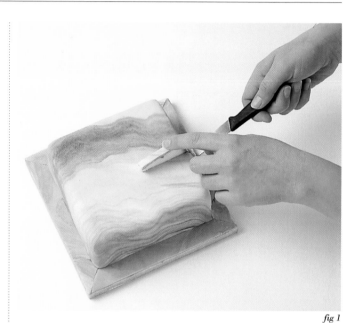

fig 1

7 Moisten the exposed cake board. Roll out the excess 'woodgrain' icing to a thickness of about 3 mm (⅛ in) and cut out four strips. Lay one strip down each edge. Trim to fit (see page 12).

8 Now make the tools (fig 2). To make the screwdriver, roll 10 g (¼ oz) of grey sugarpaste into a sausage (rope) approximately 10 cm (4 in) long and squash one end. Make a small flattened grey ball, and place this against the blunt end. Make a handle by rolling the red sugarpaste into

a pear shape. Place the screwdriver into position on the cake and adhere with a little water.

9 For the ruler, roll 20 g (¾ oz) of white sugarpaste into a flat strip and cut out a rectangle 13 cm x 2.5 cm (5 in x 1 in). Carefully paint on a few lines for markings with black food colour and a fine paint brush. Stick the ruler onto the cake.

10 To make the hammer, first roll the black sugarpaste into an exaggerated pear shape. Slice a strip off the larger end and place onto the cake board. For the handle, roll the tan sugarpaste into a slightly tapering sausage approximately 18 cm (7 in) long. Place the handle into position, and stick with a little water using the side of the cake as support.

11 For the pencil, roll the blue sugarpaste into a thin sausage about 10 cm (4 in)

fig 2

long. Stick this onto the cake board. Finish it off with a tiny cone of flesh-coloured icing and paint in a tiny point with black food colour.

12 To put the saw together, sandwich the grey blade between the two orange handles (*fig 3*). A little water should be enough to cement the sections together but if you find they won't stick, use a few dabs of royal icing. Lightly moisten the edge of the saw handle and the inside of the

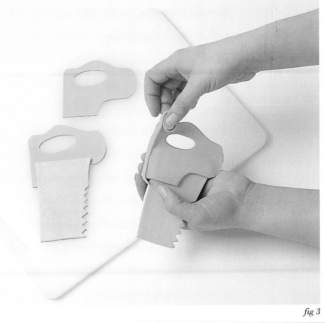

fig 3

hole. Roll out the orange sugarpaste into a strip and wind this round to neaten the appearance of the handle. Trim away any excess.

13 Put the saw into the slot.

TIP: *Make the saw at least a day before the rest of the cake so you won't have to wait for it to dry when everything else is ready.*

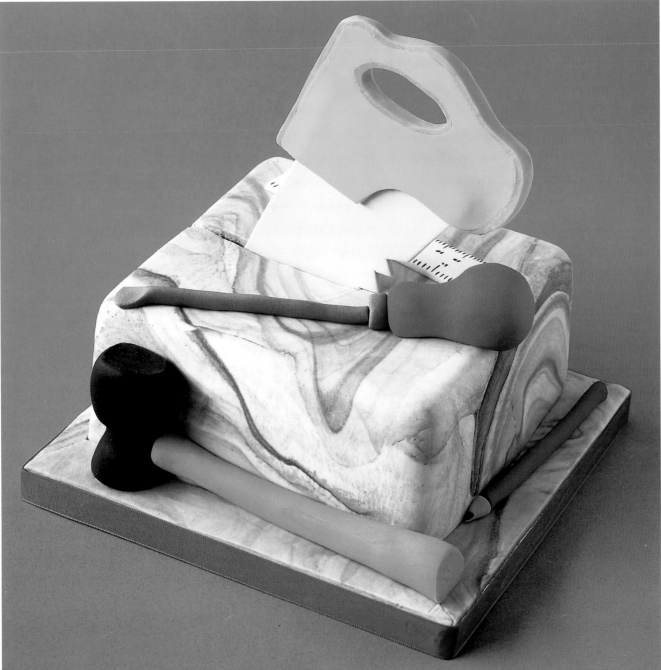

SPEND, SPEND, SPEND

A dazzling cake piled up with gold coins that would suit either an accountant or someone who just likes to spend, spend, spend! This makes a nice cake for a man and let's face it, is a lot more original than a pair of socks! If you're making it for a woman, you might like to substitute small purses for the drawstring pouches.

INGREDIENTS

18 cm (7 in) square cake
1 quantity buttercream (see page 10)
500 g (1 lb 2 oz) emerald green sugarpaste (rolled fondant icing)
100 g (4 oz) dark brown sugarpaste (rolled fondant icing)
100 g (4 oz) light brown sugarpaste (rolled fondant icing)
10 g (¼ oz) red sugarpaste (rolled fondant icing)
10 g (¼ oz) blue sugarpaste (rolled fondant icing)
About 60 foil-covered chocolate coins
1 tbsp white royal icing (see page 10)
Icing sugar, for rolling out
Water

UTENSILS

25 cm (10 in) gold-coloured square cake board
Carving knife
Small sharp knife
Palette knife (metal spatula)
Rolling pin
Cake smoothers
Paintbrush
Piping bag fitted with a No 2 nozzle (round tip)

1 Slice off the top of the cake to level it and turn it upside down on the cake board so that the base now forms the top. Position the cake so that it sits off-centre on the board.

2 Slice the cake in half and fill it with buttercream. Spread buttercream over the top and down the sides with a palette knife.

3 Knead the emerald green sugarpaste (rolled fondant icing) and roll it out. Carefully cover the cake.

4 Smooth the sugarpaste over the top and sides with your hands and trim away any excess icing at the base. Then run over the surface of the icing using a pair of cake smoothers.

5 To make a purse, take the dark brown icing and mould it into a cone shape (*fig 1*). Push your finger into the top of the thin end to make a slight hollow. This will become the opening of the purse. Pinch the edges around the top of the hollow to thin them slightly and bend them outwards. Squeeze the neck of the purse to re-shape it as necessary. Stand the purse in position on

fig 1

the cake. Repeat with the lighter brown icing but this time lay it flat on the cake instead of standing up.

6 Begin to position the coins around the cake, securing them into position with royal icing (*fig 2*).

7 Finish off the purses by adding a drawstring. Poke the pointed end of a paintbrush around the neck of each purse to leave a line of small dots. (Make approximately 6-7 holes per purse about 1 cm (½ in) apart.) Using the piping bag and No 2 nozzle (round tip), pipe a line of icing between two of the holes. Leave a gap and pipe another line between the next two holes (*fig 3*). This should give the impression of a cord being threaded through.

8 Make two tiny red balls and two tiny blue ones out of icing. Stick the two red ones on the neck of the standing up purse. Pipe two 'tails' of icing away from them. On the lying down

purse, pipe the 'tails' before adding the blue balls to look as though the purse has fallen slightly open.

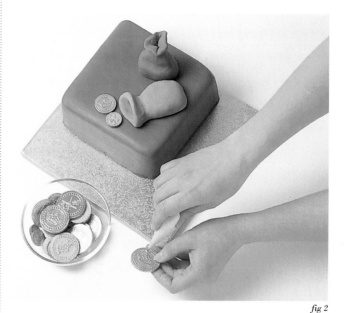

fig 2

9 Finish arranging the coins around the cake and board.

fig 3

TIP: *It's always worth stocking up with chocolate coins at Christmas when they are more readily available in the shops. You never know when you might need some!*

SHOPPING BAG

The ideal cake for anyone who shops 'til they drop. If the recipient favours a certain shop, have their bags poking out amongst the shopping. You could also paint small rectangles of icing with food colour to look like credit cards. If you really want to cheat, simply stuff the top of the bag with a couple of real (and clean!) scarves.

INGREDIENTS

18 cm (7 in) square cake
1 quantity buttercream (see page 100)
750 g (1 lb 10 oz) mid-blue sugarpaste (rolled fondant icing)
100 g (4 oz) green sugarpaste (rolled fondant icing)
150 g (5 oz) pink sugarpaste (rolled fondant icing)
100 g (4 oz) white sugarpaste (rolled fondant icing)
90 g (3 ½ oz) dark blue sugarpaste (rolled fondant icing)
90 g (3 ½ oz) yellow sugarpaste (rolled fondant icing)
90 g (3 ½ oz) red sugarpaste (rolled fondant icing)
200 g (7 oz) black sugarpaste (rolled fondant icing)
30 g (1 ¼ oz) light orange sugarpaste (rolled fondant icing)
Black food colour
Icing (confectioners') sugar, for rolling out
Water

UTENSILS

20 cm (8 in) square cake board
Carving knife
Palette knife (metal spatula)
Small sharp knife
Rolling pin
Cake smoothers
Template (see page 93)
Drinking straw
Paintbrush

fig 1

1 Lay the cake flat and cut a long tapering triangle off two opposite sides (*fig 1*). Stand the cake upright so that the shortest edge is at the top of the cake and check that it balances. If it doesn't, shave bits of cake off the bottom. Place bits of the off-cuts against the wider sides of the cake. These will look like exciting bulges when the cake is covered.

2 Place the cake diagonally on the cake board. Slice and fill the centre with buttercream. Use the buttercream to 'glue' the off-cuts to the side of the cake. Then spread the buttercream over the top and sides.

3 Knead and roll out the mid-blue sugarpaste (rolled fondant icing). Cut out a thick strip approximately 55 cm (22 in) long and 2.5 cm (1 in) deeper than the height of the

cake. Keep the excess. Starting from the back, carefully wrap the sugarpaste around the cake, making sure that the top edge of the icing is higher than the top edge of the cake. Trim and keep any excess icing from the base and neaten the top edge.

4 Begin to fill the top of the bag (*fig 2*). Make two 50 g (2 oz) green sugarpaste squares. Make a bottle out of 50 g (2 oz) pink topped with a small, slightly flattened 20 g (¾ oz) ball of white. Place these into the top of the bag and fill the empty spaces with flat squares of dark blue, yellow, red and pink sugarpaste slightly scrunched up and allowed to fall over the sides of the bag. Roll out 50 g (2 oz) white and cut out a glove

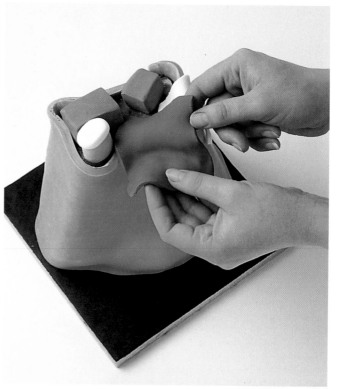

fig 2

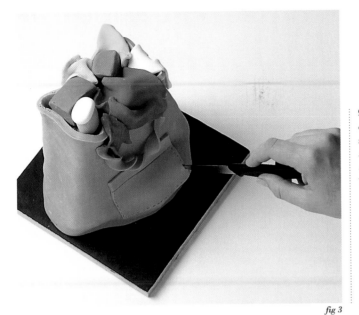

9 Cut a second glove shape out of 20 g (¾ oz) white sugarpaste. Cut out a pink and an orange square. Arrange and stick onto the board with water.

10 Make a necklace by partially mixing a tiny ball of blue and pink sugarpaste into 25 g (1 oz) of white. Roll the icing into tiny balls. Arrange in a wavy line around the board and secure. Add a small yellow oval for a clasp.

fig 3

11 Using black food colour, carefully paint small irregular oval shapes onto the orange scarf to achieve a leopard skin effect.

TIP: *When butter-creaming the cake, cover the sides of the cake first. This allows you to hold the cake steady by the top and stops you getting sticky.*

shape using the template. Insert this into the top of the bag and allow the fingers to fall over the side. Secure everything with a little water

5 Roll the remaining mid-blue sugarpaste out flat and cut out two strips about 23 cm x 2 cm (9 in x ¾ in). Twist the sugarpaste to form a handle and stick to the side of the cake with water. Repeat on the other side. Cut out a pocket and stick it to the front of the cake. Score a line using the back of a knife about 2 cm (¾ in) from the top of the pocket. Using just the tip of a sharp, pointed knife, make a line of tiny incisions around the edge of the pocket and the tops of the handles to look like stitching *(fig 3)*.

6 Decorate the pocket with a button made out of a small flattened ball of yellow. Press a drinking straw and the end of a paintbrush into the centre of the button.

7 Moisten the cake board with a little water. Roll out the black sugarpaste and cover the board in sections (see page 12). Trim the edges.

8 Make the purse out of the red sugarpaste rolled into a slightly misshapen oval. Score a few creases into the sugar-paste using the back of a knife. Stick a thin strip of yellow onto the top and two small yellow pearls for the clasp. Place against the bag.

FROG POND

In this cake, the pond is 'flooded' with royal icing. If you don't feel competent about trying this, simply cover the board with blue sugarpaste instead. The second new technique is modelling the waves out of piped royal icing. Don't worry if you're a bit unsure about handling a piping bag because the more wobbly the line the better.

INGREDIENTS

Heart-shaped cake cut out of a 18 cm (7 in) square cake using the template on page 94
1 ½ quantities buttercream (see page 10)
750 g (1 lb 10 oz) mid-green sugarpaste (rolled fondant icing)
175 g (6 oz) dark green sugarpaste (rolled fondant icing)
25 g (1 oz) yellow sugarpaste (rolled fondant icing)
25 g (1 oz) black sugarpaste (rolled fondant icing)
50 g (2 oz) white sugarpaste (rolled fondant icing)
6 tbsp royal icing (see page 10)
Pink and blue food colours
Icing (confectioners') sugar, for rolling out on
Water

UTENSILS

30 cm (12 in) round cake board
Carving knife
Small sharp knife
Palette knife (metal spatula)
Rolling pin
Cake smoothers
Cocktail stick (toothpick) or spaghetti
Piping (decorating) bag (with uncut end)
Paintbrush
Small circle cutters or icing nozzles (tips)
Piping bag (decorating) with large nozzle inside (eg No 4 or round tip)
Small bowls x 2
Small plastic bags

1 Slice the cake in half and fill the centre with buttercream. Place the cake on the board and cover the top and sides with buttercream as well.

2 Knead and roll out the mid-green sugarpaste (rolled fondant icing). Lift and place over the cake. Smooth the sides using your hands and a pair of cake smoothers and trim and keep any excess from the base.

3 Using the back of a knife, score a central vein down the centre of the leaf and add a couple leading away from it. Use about 10 g (¼ oz) of the leftover icing to make a sausage about 10 cm (4 in) long for the stem. Drape this from the back of the leaf onto the cake board.

4 Now make the frogs *(fig 1)*. Make a 50 g (2 oz) ball of dark green sugarpaste for the male frog's body. Stick this onto the edge of the leaf and insert a cocktail (toothpick) stick or couple of strands of uncooked spaghetti.

fig 1

5 Moisten the neck and stick on a 25 g (1 oz) ball of dark green sugarpaste for the head.

6 To make the mouth, roll 10 g (¼ oz) of dark green sugarpaste into a longish oval

and press a line down the centre using the back of a knife. Tweak the ends and stick onto the head.

7 Make each leg out of 10 g (¼ oz) of green sugarpaste. Roll each one into a slightly tapered 10 cm (4 in) sausage (rope). Press and flatten about 2.5 cm (1 in) of the thicker end. The leg should now look like a small paddle. Cut 2 small triangles out of the foot to give the impression of webbed feet. Bend the leg into an 'S' shape and press against the frog's body, allowing the

end of the foot to just dangle over the side of the lily leaf. Repeat with the other foot.

8 For the lady frog, again make another 25 g (1 oz) ball of dark green sugarpaste for the head. Add a 10 g (¼ oz) strip for the mouth and score a line across the middle.

9 Make four small white sugarpaste balls and stick two

onto each frog for eyes. Add a small flattened circle of black to each eye and finish with a small ball of white for a highlight.

10 Add a little strip of yellow sugarpaste for Mrs Frog's hair. Cut out a pink bow and secure this to her head with a little water.

11 Divide 15 g (½ oz) dark green sugarpaste into four and make four small sausage-shaped arms, two for each frog. Secure these in position with a little water.

fig 2

12 Make the rocks by partially kneading 25 g (1 oz) black sugarpaste into 50 g (2 oz) white. Pull bits off and roll into small misshapen ball shapes *(fig 2)*. Moisten the cake board and stick the rocks, close together, around the edge.

13 Put 5 tbsp royal icing into a small bowl. Stir in enough blue food colour to make it a

rich blue. Add just enough water so that when the knife is lifted out, the icing begins to fall back on itself and loses its shape. Spoon it into an empty piping (decorating) bag. Snip the end off the bag and starting from the pointed end of the lily, begin to fill pool with 'water'. Move the piping bag from side to side across the exposed cake board in a wiggly motion. Push the icing into any reluctant corners with the tip of a damp paint brush. Leave to dry for at least a few hours, or over night.

14 Make the lily flowers by cutting out 5 white petals per flower using a small circle cutter or piping nozzle (tip). Stick the petals around the lily pad. Now make yellow sugarpaste circles and stick these securely in the centre of each flower.

15 Put 1 tbsp white royal icing into a bag with No 4

nozzle (tip). Pipe a line around base of the lily leaf. Using a damp paintbrush, stroke the icing back away from the leaf to achieve the wave effect *(fig 3)*.

TIP: *Don't worry if you get a few trapped air bubbles in your 'flooded' water. They will enhance the pond by making it look authentic.*

fig 3

TEATIME TABLE

There are a number of ways you can cheat with this cake and yet still produce something spectacular and unique. If you don't fancy making a gelatin plate (or you haven't got the time to wait for it to dry) simply use a real one instead and pile it up with home-made (or shop-bought) goodies you know the family will love.

INGREDIENTS

20 cm (8 in) round sponge
1 quantity buttercream (see page 10)
300 g (11 oz) gelatin icing (see page 10)
550 g (1 lb 4 oz) white sugarpaste (rolled fondant icing)
750 g (1 lb 10 oz) pink sugarpaste (rolled fondant icing)
Cornflour (cornstarch)
1 tbsp white royal icing (see page 10)
Small jelly sweets (candies)
About 20 petit-four size cakes
Icing (confectioners') sugar, for rolling out on
Water

UTENSILS

30 cm (12 in) round cake board
Carving knife
Small sharp knife
Palette knife (metal spatula)
20-23 cm (8-9 in) round china plate
Rolling pin
35 cm (14 in) round cake board for use as a template
Piping (decorating) bag
Paintbrush
Clingfilm (plastic wrap)

1 Cover the china plate with clingfilm (plastic wrap) and a fine dusting of cornflour (cornstarch).

2 Roll out the gelatin icing and cover the plate. Trim the edges. Leave to dry for at least 24 hours, turning the icing plate over when it has hardened enough to support itself.

3 Level the top of the cake and turn it upside down on to the cake board. Slice it in half and fill the centre with buttercream. Reassemble the cake and spread additional buttercream around the top and sides.

4 Knead and roll out the white sugarpaste (rolled fondant icing). Place it over the cake and cover it. Smooth down the top and sides with cake smoothers and trim away any excess.

5 Knead and roll out the pink sugarpaste to a thickness of about 5mm (¼ in). Using the larger cake board or equivalent as a template, cut out a circle.

6 Lay the pink icing on top of the white and allow it to fall into folds down the sides (fig 1).

7 Using the end of a paintbrush, poke a pattern into the edges of the cloth (fig 2).

8 When the plate is dry, place it on top of the tablecloth.

fig 2

Secure it firmly with a dab of royal icing.

9 Put the royal icing into a piping (decorating) bag and snip off the end. Decorate the edge of the plate with small jelly sweets (candies). Secure them into position with the royal icing (fig 3).

10 Fill the plate with small cakes, biscuits (cookies) or whatever takes your fancy.

TIP: *To ensure that the plate does not crack when you turn it over to dry the underside, place some scrunched up clingfilm (plastic wrap) under the plate to provide support.*

fig 1

fig 3

YACHT

A fun cake for anyone who fancies themselves as a bit of a sailor. Paint the recipient's name or age on the sails and if they actually own their own boat, copy those colours. Have fun with the sea as well. Add jelly (candy) or icing fish or, if your sense of humour veers towards the wicked, maybe a shark's fin or two.

INGREDIENTS

15 cm (6 in) square cake
1 quantity buttercream (see page 10)
550 g (1 lb 3 oz) red sugarpaste (rolled fondant icing)
110 g (4 ¼ oz) black sugarpaste (rolled fondant icing)
100 g (4 oz) white sugarpaste (rolled fondant icing)
50 g (2 oz) blue sugarpaste (rolled fondant icing)
25 g (1 oz) flesh-coloured sugarpaste (rolled fondant icing)
150 g (5 oz) green sugarpaste (rolled fondant icing)
Black and blue food colours
5 tbsp royal icing (see page 10)
Icing (confectioners') sugar, for rolling out
Water

UTENSILS

25 cm (10 in) round cake board
Carving knife
Small sharp knife
Palette knife (metal spatula)
Rolling pin
Cake smoothers
Paintbrushes, one medium, one fine
Wooden skewers x 2
Small bowl
Small plastic bags
Clear sticky tape
Cardboard sail (see template on page 94)

fig 1

1 Cut out the shape of the boat from the sponge *(fig 1)*. Use strips cut from the discarded edges of the sponge to increase the boat's length. Carefully carve the sides of the cake so that they slope gently inwards and give the boat a nice rounded look. Slice and fill the centre with buttercream, then spread it around the top and sides.

2 Roll out 450 g (1 lb) red sugarpaste (rolled fondant icing) on a surface dusted with icing (confectioners') sugar. Cut out a strip approximately 50 cm (20 in) long and 5 cm (2 in) wide. (This last measurement depends on the depth of your cake so measure it first before cutting.) Roll the strip up like a bandage and starting from the straight edge at the back of the boat, unwind it around the base of the boat. Neaten the sides using smoothers and trim away any excess icing at the join (seam). Ensure that the top edge of the icing lies level with the top of the cake, trimming it if necessary.

3 To give the impression of boards around the boat, take a ruler and holding it horizontally, press the edge two or three times into both sides of the boat. (A photograph showing this technique appears in 'Enchanted House' page 34.)

4 Thinly roll out 100 g (4 oz) black sugarpaste and cut out a shape slightly larger than the top of the boat. Lay the sugarpaste on the top of the boat and run a knife around the edge to trim it to size. Roll out 100 g (4 oz) red sugarpaste and cut out two strips for the boat's seats approximately 2.5 cm (1 in) wide. Lightly moisten the black sugarpaste with a little water and place them into position.

5 Roll 100 g (4 oz) of red sugarpaste icing into a sausage about 60 cm (24 in) long. Moisten the top edge of the boat with water and lay the strip into position *(fig 2)*.

6 Shape 90 g (3 ½ oz) white sugarpaste into an oval for the sailor's body. Thinly roll out 25 g (1 oz) of blue sugarpaste and cut out three thin strips about 15 cm (6 in) long. Moisten the body and wrap them round to make stripes. Make two arms out of 25 g (1 oz) blue sugarpaste. Bend them slightly at the elbow and stick onto the body with water *(fig 3)*. Place the sailor into position and secure with a little water. For extra security, carefully push the smaller wooden skewer through the body into the cake, leaving about 2.5 cm (1 in) protruding. Roll 10 g (¼ oz) flesh-coloured sugarpaste into a ball for the head. Moisten the neck and slide the head into position over the skewer.

To make the sailor's facial hair ('de rigeuer' for any self-respecting seaman!) take the remaining black sugarpaste. Make a tiny triangle for the beard and stick on to the face.

fig 2

fig 3

Add two tiny black ovals for the moustache. Stick a small flattened circle of white sugarpaste onto the top of his head to make his cap and finish it off with a tiny white oval of icing stuck to the front

to make a peak. Add three tiny balls of flesh-coloured icing for the ears and nose and paint in the eyes, hair and a dot for the mouth with black food colour and a fine paint-brush. Finish the arms with

hands made out of two balls of flesh-coloured sugarpaste.

7 For the octopus, make a 100 g (4 oz) ball of green sugarpaste for the head and five 50 g (2 oz) green sausages (ropes) for the legs (*fig 3*).

8 Place 5 tbsp of royal icing in a bowl and partially mix in a small amount of blue food colour. Using a palette knife, swirl the icing around the cake board. Position the octopus' head and legs, making sure that the 'sea' covers the tops of the legs.

9 Stick two white circles of icing onto the octopus' face.

Add two smaller black ones. finish off with two tiny white flattened dots of white to make the highlights. Paint in a mouth and two eyebrows with black food colour.

10 Attach the sails to the second wooden skewer with sticky tape. Finally insert them into the boat.

TIP: *If you go too far mixing the blue food colour into the 'sea' and it all turns blue, don't panic! Simply add more white royal icing to reverse the process.*

BOUQUET

The wonderful thing about this cake is its versatility. Not only would it make a lovely birthday cake but it could also be used for Mother's Day, Easter, Anniversaries or Valentine's Day. These roses are the fastest and easiest you'll ever see in icing. Colour them the recipient's favourite colour or, if rushed, use silk blooms instead.

INGREDIENTS

15 cm x 20 cm (6 in x 8 in) cake (Don't rush out to buy a special tin, simply trim a 20 cm (8 in) square cake instead.)
1 quantity buttercream (see page 10)
1 kg (2 lb 4 oz) white sugarpaste (rolled fondant icing)
50 g (2 oz) pale green sugarpaste (rolled fondant icing)
50 g (2 oz) mid-green sugarpaste (rolled fondant icing)
50 g (2 oz) dark green sugarpaste (rolled fondant icing)
100 g (4 oz) yellow sugarpaste (rolled fondant icing)
25 g (1 oz) violet sugarpaste (rolled fondant icing)
2 tbsp green royal icing (see page 10)
Icing (confectioners') sugar, for rolling out
Water

UTENSILS

35 cm (12 in) square cake board
Carving knife
Small sharp knife
Palette knife (metal spatula)
Rolling pin
Wooden spoon
Clingfilm (plastic wrap)
Paintbrush
Piping (decorating) bag with No 3 nozzle (round tip)
Tin foil
Cellophane (approximately 38 cm x 43 cm/15 in x 17 in)
If you can't find cellophane in your local craft shop, buy some of the real thing from a florist instead.
Clear sticky tape
1 metre (39 in) yellow ribbon

fig 1

1 Shape the cake by slicing two long triangles off the sides and a slope into the front (*fig 1*). Place the cake diagonally onto the cake board.

2 Slice the cake in half and fill the centre with buttercream and then cover the top and sides with buttercream as well.

3 Knead and roll the white sugarpaste (rolled fondant icing) until it's about 3 mm (⅛ in) thick. Now carefully lift the icing and place over the cake, making sure that enough icing falls onto the board at the front of the cake for you to be able to make the folds later on.

4 Gather the icing up at the front and using a wooden spoon, coax the icing into folds (*fig 2*).

5 Wriggle your finger under the point at which the gathers meet the cake to make a tunnel through which you will thread

the ribbon later. Support the tunnel while it's drying by placing a bit of scrunched up clingfilm (plastic wrap) under the arch.

6 Trim and neaten the rest of the icing around the edges of the cake and secure the bits that rest on the board with a little water.

7 Make the leaves by rolling out about half of one of the green sugarpastes. Using a the tip of a sharp knife, cut out a simple leaf shape. Turn the knife over and press the back of it into the leaf to make a couple of simple veins. Place the leaf on a bit of partially crumpled tin (aluminium) foil so that it dries in a slightly irregular shape. Repeat with the other green sugarpastes, making a total of about fifty leaves in all.

8 To make the roses, take a 10 g (¼ oz) ball of yellow sugarpaste and roll it into a

fig 2

strip about 15 cm (6 in) long. Paint a line of water down the centre of the strip and roll it up (not too tightly) like a miniature Swiss roll. Tweak the rose into a point at the base and carefully bend back

fig 3

the top of the rose petals *(fig 3)*. Put a tiny ball of yellow sugarpaste to one side to make the iris centres later and use the rest to make a further eleven roses. Leave them to dry on their sides.

9 For the irises, take a pea-sized ball of violet sugarpaste and press it into a flat oval shape. Dab a little water in the centre and fold the icing almost in half. Bend the two ends back slightly and tweak the base into a point. Stick a tiny ball of yellow into the centre and place to dry on its side. Make another nine irises.

10 Place two tablespoons of green royal icing into a piping

bag fitted with a No 3 nozzle (round tip). Starting from just inside the folds at the front of the cake, pipe about eight flower stems.

11 Beginning from the top of the cake and working down, stick the roses and leaves into position with the royal icing.

12 Insert the irises into any gaps.

13 Tidy up any dusty icing (confectioners') sugar smudges with a damp paintbrush.

14 Place the cellophane over the cake. Secure the far end of the cellophane to the cake board with a couple of small

pieces of clear sticky tape. Gather the rest up at the front.

15 Thread the ribbon through the hole and tie a neat bow over the top of the cellophane.

16 Tweak the cellophane into place and secure at the sides with sticky tape.

TIP: *To give your bouquet that final touch, buy a card from a real florist complete with its own miniature envelope. Write your message and tuck it into the bow.*

RACETRACK

A fun race track suitable for boys (or girls!) from eight to eighty. To make it a little more personal, paint 'Birthday Boy's' age on the winning car (or perhaps the losing one if he's really depressed about the relentless passing of the years!) and model it in his favourite colour or those of his favoured racing team.

INGREDIENTS

20 cm x 18 cm (8 in x 7 in)
cake (trim down an 20 cm
(8 in) square cake)
1 quantity buttercream (see
page 10)
1.15 kg (2 lb 6 oz) mid-green
sugarpaste (rolled fondant
icing)
10 g (¼ oz) red sugarpaste
(rolled fondant icing)
10 g (¼ oz) blue sugarpaste
(rolled fondant icing)
10 g (¼ oz) yellow sugarpaste
(rolled fondant icing)
25 g (1 oz) black sugarpaste
(rolled fondant icing)
25 g (1 oz) white sugarpaste
(rolled fondant icing)
100 g (4 oz) grey sugarpaste
(rolled fondant icing)
100 g (4 oz) dark green
sugarpaste (rolled fondant
icing)
Black food colour
Icing (confectioners') sugar,
for rolling out
Water

UTENSILS

25 cm (10 in) square cake
board
Carving knife
Small sharp knife
Palette knife (metal spatula)
Rolling pin
Cake smoothers
Drinking straw
Paintbrushes, one medium,
one fine
Wooden skewer trimmed to a
length of about 13 cm (5 in)
Sieve (strainer)
Small plastic bags

1 Slice off the top of the cake to level it if necessary and place the cake upside down on the board. Cut the cake in half and fill the middle with buttercream. Coat the top and sides of the cake with buttercream as well.

2 Dust your work surface with icing (confectioners') sugar and roll out 1 kg (2 lb 4 oz) of the mid-green sugarpaste (rolled fondant icing) into a thick rectangle approximately 33 cm x 28 cm (13 in x 11 in) and about 8 mm (¼ in) thick.

3 Lift the icing and cover the cake. Smooth down the sides using your hands first and then the smoothers. Trim away and keep the excess to make bushes later.

fig 1

4 Cover the exposed cake board using the remaining mid-green icing cut into four strips (see page 12 for details how to do this).

5 For the cars, roll the red, blue and yellow sugarpaste

into three tapered carrot shapes, each about 5 cm (2 in) long. Cut a small slice off the back of each car and re-shape these cut off bits into three small rectangles and put them to one side.

Take 10 g (¼ oz) black sugarpaste and roll it into a sausage (rope) about 7.5 cm (3 in) long. Divide this into 12 equal slices and model each slice into a small flattish round shape to make the wheels. Stick four wheels onto each car with water. Add details to the wheels by pressing the tip of a drinking straw into the centre of each wheel to leave a ring. Then make a small dot with the wooden end of a paintbrush in the middle of the ring (*fig 1*).

Stick a pea-sized ball of white sugarpaste onto the top

of each racing car, about 1 cm (½ in) from the back end. Stick three tiny flattened black sugarpaste ovals onto the front of the helmets to make visors. Stick the three coloured rectangles onto the car behind the helmets.

fig 2

6 For the racetrack, roll out 100 g (4 oz) grey sugarpaste and cut out a rectangle about 30 cm x 7.5 cm (12 in x 3 in). Lay this diagonally across the cake and fix into position with water. Trim away any excess icing from the corners.

Knead and roll out the remaining white sugarpaste and cut out a rectangle 10 cm x 5 cm (4 in x 2 in). Place the wooden skewer into position at a slight angle. Moisten the edge of the cake and the top half of the skewer slightly with a little water. Carefully wrap one edge of the flag round the skewer and allow the rest of the icing to drape elegantly over the side of the cake, hiding the edge of the road (*fig 2*). Paint a chequered design onto the flag using black food colour and a fine paintbrush.

7 Now make the bushes. Put the dark green sugarpaste and any remaining mid-green sugarpaste together but don't knead them together. Pull off a lump of the icing and push it through a sieve (strainer) (*fig 3*). Slice off the strands with a knife and position the 'bush' on the base of the cake, sticking them down with a little water. Continue to do this all round the base of the cake and onto the top too. (This is an extremely effective way to disguise any cracks or blemishes in the icing!)

Make another six small wheels out of the remaining black sugarpaste. Press a tiny ball of grey into the centre of each one and stack them into two piles. Position one pile each side of the track. Using black food colour, paint a

fig 3

number onto each car and lines down the centre of the track. Fix the cars into position with water and paint two skid marks behind the car veering off the track using the medium paintbrush and slightly watered down food colour.

TIP: *If you want to make things easier for yourself, either substitute toy cars for the icing ones or buy some car-shaped sweets.*

GOLF COURSE

Poor old Mister Mole. He'd just found a nice ready-made hole and had settled down for a sleep in when a nasty white thing landed on his head! This cake is easier to put together than it looks. The cake can be as irregular as you like and the shrubbery can be used to hide any imperfections in the icing.

INGREDIENTS

23 cm (9 in) round cake
1 ½ quantities buttercream (see page 10)
1 kg (2 lb 4 oz) green sugarpaste (rolled fondant icing)
70 g (2 ¾ oz) black sugarpaste (rolled fondant icing)
25 g (1 oz) dark grey sugarpaste (rolled fondant icing)
100 g (4 oz) white sugarpaste (rolled fondant icing)
100 g (4 oz) darker green sugarpaste (rolled fondant icing)
Silver and black food colours
2 tsp light golden sugar
Icing (confectioners') sugar, for rolling out
Water

UTENSILS

25 cm (10 in) square cake board
Carving knife
Small sharp knife
Palette knife (metal spatula)
Rolling pin
Cake smoothers
Paintbrushes, one medium, one fine
Ball tool or wooden spoon
Two cocktail sticks (toothpicks), optional
Sieve (strainer)
Small plastic bags

fig 1

fig 2

1 Slice the top off the cake to level it if necessary and place it upside down on the cake board. Carve away part of the sides of the cake so that it now forms a slightly irregular shape. Cut out a hole slightly towards the rear of the cake approximately 5 cm (2 in) wide and 2.5 cm (1 in) deep (*fig 1*). Slice and fill the centre of the cake with buttercream. Reassemble the cake and spread a thin layer of buttercream around the sides and top.

2 Knead and roll out the of green sugarpaste (rolled fondant icing) to a thickness of about 1 cm (½ in). Carefully lift it and place over the cake. Smooth over the top and sides, first with your hands, then with a pair of smoothers. Don't worry if the icing tears when you're pushing it into the hole as this will be hidden by the mole's body later. Trim away the excess icing (there should be about 300 g/11 oz). Store it in a plastic bag for making bushes later.

3 Now make the mole by rolling 50 g (2 oz) black sugarpaste into a ball and place this into the hole. Make a head by moulding the dark grey sugarpaste into a cone shape. Stick this onto the mole's body with a little water, making sure that the thinnest part of the cone is facing forwards.

Roll 10 g (¼ oz) white sugarpaste into a thin sausage (rope) approximately 15 cm (6 in) long. Lightly moisten the edge of the hole with a little water and lay the strip around the top edge and mole's body (*fig 2*). Paint a disgruntled expression onto the mole's face using black food colour and a fine paintbrush.

Add two small tapering sausages of black sugarpaste for arms. Position one as though he is rubbing his eye and the other resting on the ground.

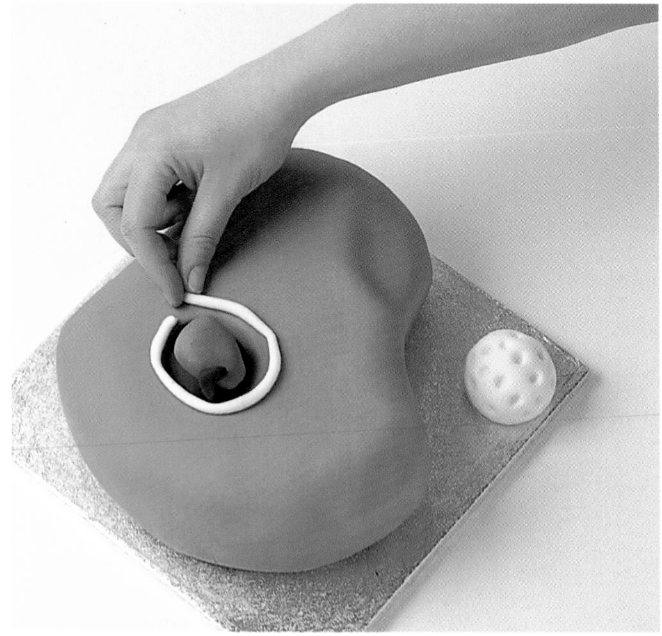

4 To make the golf ball, roll 50 g (2 oz) white sugarpaste into a ball. Using either a ball tool or the end of a wooden spoon handle, poke small dents around the outside of the ball. Stick the ball into position.

5 For the golf club, make the metal part of the golf club out of 40 g (1 ½ oz) white sugarpaste shaped into a sort of 'L' shape. Flatten and round the edges of the base part and press a few horizontal lines into the still soft sugarpaste using the back of a knife. Make a handle out of 10 g (¼ oz) black sugarpaste rolled into a sausage. Make a few diagonal indented lines across the handle and finish with a few small holes made with the end of a paintbrush (*fig 3*). Place the golf club into

fig 3

position on the cake and paint the white metal section with silver food colour.

6 Lightly moisten the exposed cake board with a little water. Press about 200 g (7 oz) of the remaining green sugarpaste

around the board, forming small undulating slopes. Trim the edges.

7 Partially mix together the remaining mid-green sugarpaste and the dark green sugarpaste. Pull off a small ball and push it through a sieve (strainer). Cut and lift the strands of sugarpaste away from the sieve with a sharp knife and place onto the cake, sticking into place with a little water. Continue around the sides of the cake hiding the joins and any blemishes in the icing as you go.

8 Moisten the bunker area with a little water. Carefully spoon about two teaspoons of light golden (brown) sugar onto the board. Brush away any stray bits of sugar with a dry paintbrush.

TIP: *If the golf ball won't stay in position on the mole's head, remove the ball and insert two cocktail sticks (toothpicks) into the mole's head, leaving about 2.5 cm (1 in) protruding. Then place the ball back in position. The cocktail sticks will provide additional support, but please ensure that nobody tries to eat the mole without removing them first.*

N.B. *Please note that the silver food colour is inedible and therefore the golf club should be discarded when cutting the cake.*

SPECIAL OCCASIONS

A special occasion deserves a special cake and
this section contains eight reasons for celebrating
and one for anyone who celebrated too much the
day before! Amongst the cakes are ideas for
Christmas, suggestions for Valentine's Day and a
simple-yet-effective cake for a wedding.

PASSING EXAMS

A cake that shows how proud you are of someone's academic achievements. You could also write their name or the subject they passed on the certificate. If you can't get hold of ready-coloured black sugarpaste and have to colour your own, invest in some disposable polythene gloves to save discolouring your hands.

INGREDIENTS

18 cm (7 in) round cake
1 quantity buttercream (see page 10)
400 g (14 oz) white sugarpaste (rolled fondant icing)
900 g (2 lb) black sugarpaste (rolled fondant icing)
50 g (2 oz) red sugarpaste (rolled fondant icing)
100 g (4 oz) green sugarpaste (rolled fondant icing)
10 g (¼ oz) yellow sugarpaste (rolled fondant icing)
10 g (¼ oz) blue sugarpaste (rolled fondant icing)
Paprika
Dark brown food colour
Icing (confectioners') sugar, for rolling out
Water

UTENSILS

30 cm (12 in) round cake board
20 cm (8 in) thin, square cake board
Spare cake board
Carving knife
Small sharp knife
Palette knife (metal spatula)
Rolling pin
Cake smoothers
Fish slice (pancake turner)
Paintbrush
Cocktail stick (toothpick)
Small plastic bags

1 Knead paprika and dark brown food colour into 250 g (9 oz) white sugarpaste (rolled fondant icing) to achieve the wood grain effect as shown on page 12.

2 Moisten the 30 cm (12 in) cake board and cover it with the 'wood' icing (see page 11). Put the board to one side.

3 Turn the cake upside down on a spare cake board or clean work surface (countertop) and round the edges with a carving knife. Place the thinner cake board on top just to check that it sits nice and flat.

4 Slice the cake in half and fill the centre with buttercream. Cover the top and sides with buttercream.

5 Knead and roll out 500 g (1 lb 2 oz) of black sugarpaste and cover the cake with it. Smooth and trim away any excess.

6 Moisten the thin cake board with a little water. Roll out the remaining black sugarpaste and use this to cover the board.

7 Lift the round base cake using a fish slice or equivalent and place in the centre of the covered cake board.

8 Lightly moisten the top of the cake and place the thin black cake board into position on the top (fig 1).

9 Make a scroll out of 150 g (5 oz) white sugarpaste. Knead and roll it out and cut out a rectangle about 18 cm x 13 cm (7 in x 5 in) long. Roll it up and stick it onto the board with a little water.

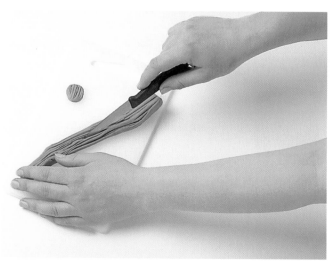

fig 2

10 Cut out two thin red strips of sugarpaste and stick onto the scroll. Add a bow made out of another two red strips folded into two loops, two 'tails' and a small strip to cover the centre (fig 2).

11 Take the green sugarpaste. Pull off a small ball and put it to one side. Roll the rest into a tapering sausage (rope) shape approximately 23 cm (9 in) long. Flatten the sausage slightly and score lines down its length using the back of a knife (fig 3). Moisten the top of the mortar board and lay the tassel upon it, allowing the icing to rest on the board at the base. Add a few thin strings of green sugarpaste to look like 'stragglers'.

12 Put the leftover ball of green sugarpaste on top and again score lines in it with the back of a knife.

13 For the pencils, simply roll the yellow sugarpaste and blue sugarpaste into 12 cm (5 in) lengths. Add a tiny brown cone to one end and a tiny flattened ball of white to the other. Paint in the leads with black food colour.

TIP: *Clean away dusty icing (confectioners') sugar fingerprints with clean water and a damp paintbrush.*

fig 1

fig 3

HALLOWE'EN SPIDER

A couple of local children gave me some hints about how to make this cake more ghoulish. Although I ignored their suggestions as they were too gory, this cake does harbour one horrible surprise. Before it was cooked, the cake was coloured an awful mouldy colour with food colours. It looked bad enough to eat!

INGREDIENTS

18 cm (7 in) round cake
1 quantity buttercream (see page 10)
450 g (1 lb) green sugarpaste (rolled fondant icing)
750 g (1 lb 10 oz) black sugarpaste (rolled fondant icing)
110 g (4 ¼ oz) white sugarpaste (rolled fondant icing)
25 g (1 oz) red sugarpaste (rolled fondant icing)
10 g (¼ oz) grey sugarpaste (rolled fondant icing)
2 liquorice (licorice) bootlaces (about 1 m/39 in long)
Red food colour
Icing (confectioners') sugar, for rolling out
Water

UTENSILS

35 cm (12 in) round cake board
Spare cake board
Carving knife
Small sharp knife
Palette knife (metal spatula)
Rolling pin
Cake smoothers
Pastry brush
Fish slice (pancake turner)
Paintbrushes, one medium, one fine
Two cocktail sticks (toothpicks), optional

1 Cover the cake board with the green sugarpaste (rolled fondant icing) (see page 11). Put to one side.

2 Place the cake onto the spare cake board and carefully carve it into a rounded dome shape.

3 Slice the cake in half and fill the centre with buttercream. Spread additional buttercream around the outside.

4 Knead and roll out the black sugarpaste to a thickness of about 5 mm (¼ in). Lift and cover the cake. Pat down and smooth the sides

fig 2

fig 1

with your hands, then run a pair of cake smoothers over the surface to make the spider become nice and rounded. Trim and keep the excess.

5 Lift the cake using a fish slice (pancake turner) or equivalent utensil and place it into the centre of the covered cake board (*fig 1*).

6 Roll and divide 100 g (4 oz) of white sugarpaste into two balls. Then slightly flatten each one to a width of about 5 cm (2 in). Stick these on with a little water to make his eyes.

7 Roll out 10 g (¼ oz) of black sugarpaste to a thickness of about 3 mm (⅛ in). Cut out two circles 3 cm (1 ¼ in) diameter. Stick these onto the whites of the eyes with a little water. Flatten two tiny white balls and stick one onto each black circle to make the highlights.

8 Roll 10 g (¼ oz) of dark grey sugarpaste into a sausage (rope) 5 cm (2 in) long. Cut in two and mould each half into an 'S' shape to make the eyebrows. Stick these into place with water (*fig 2*).

9 Thinly roll out the red sugarpaste and cut out a crescent shape for the mouth. Stick it onto the spider's face.

10 Flatten 10 g (¼ oz) of white sugarpaste and cut out two triangles for the spider's teeth. Line up the top of each tooth with the top of the mouth and allow them to fall into a curved shape.

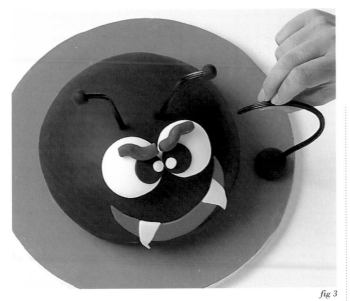

fig 3

11 Now divide the liquorice (licorice) bootlaces into eight even 20 cm (8 in) lengths for the legs and two 7.5 cm (3 in) lengths to make the spider's antennae.

12 Take 100 g (4 oz) of the leftover black sugarpaste and divide this into eight balls.

13 Moisten the base of one of the balls and position on the board. Poke one of the liquorice legs into the ball then bend it back and insert it into the spider's body. Repeat with the other seven legs (*fig 3*).

14 Stick a little ball of black sugarpaste onto one end of both liquorice antennae. Make two small holes in the top of the spider's head and insert the liquorice.

15 Paint tiny blood vessels onto the eyes with red food colour and a fine paintbrush.

16 Finally tidy up any icing (confectioners') sugar smudges with a damp paintbrush.

TIP: *If you find the antennae won't stand up, insert a cocktail stick (toothpick) up the middle of each bit of bootlace to add support. Ensure that they are removed when the cake is cut.*

VALENTINE LIPS

If, as they say, the way to a man's (or woman's) heart is through their stomach, what better way to get there than by presenting them with this stylish, eye-catching cake. Gold cake boards are easily available from cake decorating equipment shops, and really set off the black and red icing.

INGREDIENTS

25 cm (10 in) square cake
2 quantities of buttercream (see page10)
1.25 kg (2 lb 12 oz) red sugarpaste (rolled fondant icing)
50 g (2 oz) black sugarpaste (rolled fondant icing)
1 tbsp black royal icing (see page 10)
Icing (confectioners') sugar, for rolling out
Water

UTENSILS

30 cm (12 in) square gold cake board
Cake template (see page 94)
Carving knife
Small sharp knife
Palette knife (metal spatula)
Rolling pin
Cake smoothers
Small heart-shaped cutter
Piping (decorating) bag and No 3 piping nozzle (round tip)
Paintbrush

fig 1

1 Cut out the cake using the template as a guide *(fig 1)*.

2 Round the sides and make sure that the outside edges of the lips slope downwards towards the board. Cut a groove along the middle *(fig 2)*. Position the cake on the board.

3 Slice and fill the centre with buttercream. Reassemble and cover the outside of the cake with buttercream.

4 Knead and roll out all the red sugarpaste (rolled fondant icing) to a thickness of 1 cm (½ in). (If it's nice and thick, it's easier to achieve a nice smooth luxurious finish.)

5 Lift and place the icing over the cake. Carefully press the icing into the groove. Then smooth and trim the sides,

keeping the excess icing. Finish off by running over the cake with a pair of smoothers.

6 Cut out two red heart shapes and make three sets of lips out of the leftover icing *(fig 3)*. For each pair of lips make two small red sausage (rope) shapes the same size. Make a small dent in the middle of the top lid and press the two sections together. Tweak the ends into points.

7 Thinly roll out the black sugarpaste and cut out eleven heart shapes using the cutter.

8 Arrange the hearts and lips around the cakes with squiggles of black royal icing.

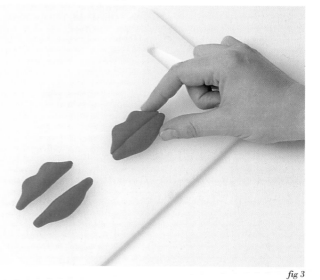
fig 3

TIP: *To save you time and effort on baking day, the small decorative lips and the hearts can easily be made a few days in advance. Store them carefully in an airtight tin until required.*

fig 2

WEDDING PRESENT

A bold way to decorate a single-tier cake. Tie the colours of the ribbons and mice in with the wedding colours and if you really fancy a challenge, find out what the bride and groom will be wearing and dress the mice in miniature replica outfits. Cake smoothers are essential for achieving the straight edges and neat corners required on this cake.

INGREDIENTS

30 cm (12 in) square fruit cake
2.5 kg (5 lb) marzipan
(almond paste)
3.25 kg (7 lb 4 oz) white
sugarpaste (rolled fondant
icing)
65 g (2 ½ oz) pink sugarpaste
(rolled fondant icing)
25 g (1 oz) black sugarpaste
(rolled fondant icing)
4 tbsp brandy
4 tbsp warmed apricot jam
White royal icing (see page 10)
Icing (confectioners') sugar
for rolling out
Black food colour
Water

UTENSILS

40 cm (16 in) square cake
board
Small sharp knife
Carving knife
Cocktail stick (toothpick)
Pastry brush
Rolling pin
Cake smoothers
Ruler
Heart-shaped cutters
Scissors
3 m (40 in) x 45 mm (1 ¾ in)
wide white ribbon
3 m (40 in) x 35 mm (1 ¼ in)
wide pink ribbon
3 m (40 in) x 25 mm (1 in) wide
white ribbon
3 m (40 in) x 15 mm (½ in) wide
pink ribbon
Piping bag
Paintbrushes, one medium,
one fine
Templates for mice clothes
(see page 94)

1 Level the top of the cake and place it upside down on the cake board. If there is a gap between what is now the base of the cake and the board, fill this with a sausage (rope) of marzipan (see page 12). Pierce the cake a number of times with the cocktail stick (toothpick) and drizzle the brandy over the cake. Brush the warmed apricot jam over the top and sides using a pastry brush.

2 Place the marzipan onto a surface dusted with icing (confectioners') sugar. Knead it until it becomes nice and pliable then roll it out and cover the cake. Stroke the marzipan into place with your hands and trim away any excess from the base. Then run a pair of cake smoothers over the top and sides trying to get the corners as neat and squared as possible.

3 Moisten the marzipan with a little water to prepare for the next step.

4 Roll out 2.5 kg (5 lb) white sugarpaste. Lift the icing and carefully place it onto the cake. Smooth and trim the sides as necessary.

5 To make the folds in the paper, carefully press a long 'V' shape into two opposite sides of the cake using the edge of a clean ruler.

6 Press a heart-shaped cutter into the icing while it's still soft. This will make the pattern on the 'paper'. Take care not to press right into the fruit cake below as moisture from the fruit could leak through and discolour the cake *(fig 1)*.

fig 1

7 Measure the height and width of the cake and cut two strips of the widest ribbon to that length (counting the height measurement twice). Arrange the two ribbons in a criss-cross fashion across the cake and secure the centre and the ends with dabs of royal icing. Don't worry if moisture from the icing leaks through the ribbon as this will be hidden by the bow and the icing round the board later. Repeat this procedure with the other three ribbon widths *(fig 2)*.

8 To cover the board, thinly roll out 850 g (1 lb 14 oz) of white sugarpaste (see page 11). Cut this into strips wider than the width of the board. Moisten the exposed cake board with a little water. Take one of the strips and lay it onto the board, deliberately allowing it to fall into folds and creases as you do so. Continue to do this all around the cake, remembering to hide the ends of the ribbon. Trim away the excess from the edges and press down any gaping holes with your thumb.

9 To make the groom, knead and roll 25 g (1 oz) pink sugarpaste into a cone shape (*fig 3*). Bend the pointed end over to make a nose and flatten the base. Knead and roll out 10 g (¼ oz) black sugarpaste and cut out a jacket shape using the template if necessary. Wrap it around the groom's back and stick with a little water. Make a tiny black sausage for the arm and cut a tiny pea-sized ball of black sugarpaste in half for his feet. Give the groom a hat made out of a small black circle topped with a small black circle of icing.

10 For the bride, mould 20 g (¾ oz) of white sugarpaste into a small cone. Take another 10 g (¼ oz) oval of white sugarpaste and place this on top. Place a small pink pointed cone shape on top of this for her head. Make a small pink sausage of icing for the bride's arms and stick this onto the front of her body in a 'U' shape. Stick three tiny white balls onto her 'hands' and indent each ball with the tip of a paintbrush.

11 Give the bride a veil (see template on page 94) cut out of a rolled out bit of white icing. Stick this to the back of her head and finish off with three tiny white balls of icing on top.

Give each mouse two tiny balls for ears and indent each one with the tip of a paintbrush. On the faces, give each mouse two small flattened white circles for eyes and an even tinier one for the nose. Paint in the mouth, eyeballs and eyelashes with black food colour and a fine paintbrush.

12 Place the two mice into position and make two tails out of 20 g (¾ oz) of pink icing. Stick these into position.

13 Arrange the rest of the ribbon into an attractive bow and stick in place with a little royal icing.

TIP: *Wipe your hands after using the black sugarpaste so you don't get dirty fingerprints everywhere.*

fig 3

VALENTINE TEDDIES

Teddies are extremely useful because they can be used on so many cakes. For example, a couple of brightly coloured ones would be ideal for a child whilst a big surly blue one bedecked with a tie might make a good gift for Father's Day. Although the ones featured here are fairly basic, you could always add some extra features.

INGREDIENTS

18 cm (7 in) square cake
1 quantity buttercream (see page 10)
750 g (1 lb 10 oz) red sugarpaste (rolled fondant icing)
150 g (5 oz) pink sugarpaste (rolled fondant icing)
350 g (12 oz) white sugarpaste (rolled fondant icing)
2 small heart-shaped chocolates
Black food colour
Icing (confectioners') sugar, for rolling out
Water

UTENSILS

25 cm (10 in) round cake board
Template (see page 94)
Carving knife
Small sharp knife
Palette knife (metal spatula)
Rolling pin
Cake smoothers
Paintbrushes, one medium, one fine
Small heart-shaped cutter

fig 1

1 Cut the cake to shape using the template (*fig 1*). Level the top and place the cake upside down in the middle of the cake board.

2 Slice the cake and fill the centre with buttercream. Reassemble the cake and spread additional buttercream around the top and sides.

3 Knead and roll out the red sugarpaste (rolled fondant icing) fairly thickly. (Don't roll it any thinner than 1 cm (½ in).) Lift and place the icing over the cake and smooth the sides and trim away the excess. Run over the top and sides with cake smoothers.

4 To make the teddies, knead 75 g (3 oz) pink sugarpaste until pliable. Pull off a small ball (just enough to make four tiny ears later) and put this to one side. Divide the rest into two cone shapes. Bend them slightly so that they lean together. Add two 10 g (¼ oz) balls for heads.

For the legs, roll a 20 g (¾ oz) lump of sugarpaste into a sausage (rope) about 13 cm (5 in) long. Divide this into four. Flatten one end of each leg to make a foot and bend the foot up slightly to form a sort of 'L' shape. Lightly squeeze the thigh and place the legs into position. Poke the pointed end of a paintbrush, into the base of each paw four times to make the pads of the feet (*fig 2*).

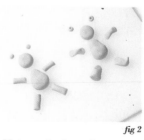

fig 2

5 Moisten the bears' stomachs with a little water and gently press the chocolates into position. Roll 10 g (¼ oz) pink icing into a sausage about 13 cm (5 in) long. Divide into four arms. Squeeze both ends

of each arm and stick onto the bodies with the hands clasping the chocolates (*fig 3*). Give both teddies two small balls of pink for ears and poke a small hole in each one with the end of a paintbrush. Paint two small circles for eyes using black food colour and a fine paintbrush. Add pupils and also eyelashes on the lady. Stick two small flattened balls of white below the eyes for the muzzle. Paint a nose and mouth on each one.

fig 3

6 Roll a 50 g (2 oz) lump of white sugarpaste into small balls. Use these to decorate the edge of the cake. Stick them in place with water. Position the teddies. Roll out 100 g (4 oz) white sugarpaste and cut out 6 hearts with the cutter. Use these to decorate the cake.

7 Moisten the exposed cake board with water. Thinly roll out 200 g (7 oz) white sugarpaste. Cut this into strips and drape onto the board, coaxing the icing into irregular folds like material. Trim away the excess and press down any unsightly bits (see page 11).

TIP: *Assemble the teddies away from the cake so you don't lean on, and damage, the surface.*

CHRISTMAS STOCKING

Just when everyone thinks that they've had all their surprises for the day, present this cake and wait for the gasps of admiration. If you have the time (usually in very short supply just before Christmas!) you could make small icing models for all the family and substitute them for the presents.

INGREDIENTS

15 cm (6 in) square fruit cake
900 g (2 lb) red sugarpaste
(rolled fondant icing)
275 g (10 oz) green sugarpaste
(rolled fondant icing)
500 g (1 lb 2 oz) white
sugarpaste (rolled fondant
icing)
3 tbsp brandy
3 tbsp apricot jam
725 g (1 lb 10 oz) marzipan
(almond paste)
26 edible gold balls
1 tsp red royal icing
(see page 10)
Icing (confectioners') sugar,
for rolling out
Water

UTENSILS

30 cm (12 in) gold-coloured
square cake board
Carving knife
Small sharp knife
Cocktail stick (toothpick)
Pastry brush
Rolling pin
Cake smoothers
Small holly cutter
Icing nozzle (tip)
Piping (decorating) bag fitted
with No 1 nozzle (round tip)
Small plastic bags for storing
icing

fig 1

1 Cut the cake in two so that one section measures 9 cm x 15 cm (3 ½ in x 6 in) and the other 7 cm x 15 cm (2 ½ in x 6 in). Place the thinner of the two strips at the base of the thicker one to produce the basic stocking shape *(fig 1)*. Cut small triangles away from the toe and heel of the stocking and also run a knife along the edges of the cake to make them rounded. Cut a slice about 2.5 cm (1 in) off the top of the cake to make the proportions look right and discard this piece.

2 Pierce the cake several times with a cocktail stick (toothpick) and drizzle the brandy over the cake. Allow the brandy to sink in, then place the cake onto the cake board.

3 Using a pastry brush, 'paint' the cake with warmed apricot jam.

4 Knead the marzipan (almond paste) on a surface dusted with icing (confectioners') sugar until it's nice and pliable. Roll it out into a rectangle approximately 5 mm (¼ in) thick and lift it over the cake. Ease it gently into position and trim away any excess marzipan. Run over the surface with cake smoothers.

5 Moisten the marzipan with a little water.

6 Knead and roll out 700 g (1 lb 8 oz) red sugarpaste (rolled fondant icing). Lay this carefully over the marzipan. Trim away the excess and keep this for modelling the presents later. Neaten the top and sides of the stocking with cake smoothers.

fig 2

7 For the presents, you will need 200 g (7 oz) of red sugarpaste, 220 g (8 oz) of green sugarpaste and 100 g (4 oz) of white *(fig 2)*. Make two 50 g (2 oz) red squares for presents, a green and white ball, using about 50 g (2 oz) of both green and white. Then make a completely green 50 g (2 oz) ball.

For the candy canes, roll out two 25 g (1 oz) sausages (ropes) of contrasting coloured icing. Twist the two sausages together and bend into a walking stick shape. Make three. Keep two back and pile the other one and the presents and balls up against the top of stocking, securing them with a little water.

8 Knead and roll 400 g (14 oz) white sugarpaste into a strip about 25 cm (10 in) long and about 13 cm (5 in) wide. Moisten the top of the stocking and lay the cuff into position so that it overlaps the presents slightly. Hold a piping nozzle (tip) at a slight angle and press it into the white to leave impressions in the still soft icing.

9 Slot the last two candy canes into position and secure with water.

10 Stick small flattened balls of white sugarpaste onto one of the red parcels to decorate it.

11 Thinly roll out 50 g (2 oz) green icing and cut out 26 holly leaves with a cutter.

Stick these onto the cake in pairs and press the back of a knife into each one three times to make veins *(fig 3)*.

12 Attach two gold balls beneath each pair of leaves using the red royal icing in the piping (decorating) bag and two tiny balls of red icing beneath the leaves on the cuff.

TIP: *To take a lot of the hard work out of kneading marzipan (almond paste), heat it in a microwave for a few seconds. However, don't overdo it or the oil in the centre will get very hot and could give you a nasty burn.*

fig 3

CHRISTMAS CRACKERS

This novel way of decorating an ordinary square fruit cake should tempt even the most turkey-stuffed palate on Christmas afternoon. You could decorate the board with small gifts appropriate to your guests or arrange real crackers around them to make a stunning centrepiece for the Christmas table.

INGREDIENTS

18 cm (7 in) square fruit cake
150 g (5 oz) black sugarpaste
(rolled fondant icing)
400 g (14 oz) red sugarpaste
(rolled fondant icing)
400 g (14 oz) green sugarpaste
(rolled fondant icing)
4 tbsp brandy
3 tbsp apricot jam
1 kg (2 lb 4 oz) marzipan
(almond paste)
1 tbsp white royal icing (see
page 10)
Icing (confectioners') sugar,
for rolling out
Water

UTENSILS

30 cm (12 in) gold-coloured
square cake board
Carving knife
Small sharp knife
Cocktail stick (toothpick)
Pastry brush
Rolling pin
Cake smoothers
Clingfilm (plastic wrap)
Paintbrush
No 3 piping nozzle (round tip)
Piping (decorating) bag fitted
with No 1 nozzle (round tip)
2 m (2 yards 7 in) tartan
ribbon
Fish slice (pancake turner)

fig 1

fig 2

7 Moisten the ends of the cracker with water. Roll out 200 g (7 oz) red sugarpaste and cut out two strips about 20 cm x 7.5 cm (8 in x 3 in) Serrate one edge and wind around one end of the cracker (*fig 2*). Press the back of a knife into the icing a few times to make creases and tweak the jagged edges so that they stand out slightly. If they keep flopping, support them with a ball of scrunched up clingfilm (plastic wrap) until they dry.

1 Cut the cake into two 5 cm (2 in) strips. Use the remaining cake to extend the length of the first two strips (*fig 1*). Run a knife along the two long edges of each cracker to slightly round them.

2 Pierce both cakes a few times using a cocktail stick and pour the brandy over the holes.

3 Cover both crackers with a pastry brush dipped into warmed apricot jam.

4 Dust your work surface with a little icing (confectioners') sugar and knead 500 g (1 lb 2 oz) marzipan (almond paste) until

pliable. Smooth down the marzipan using your hands and a pair of cake smoothers and trim away any excess. Press a finger round the cracker to make a dent about 5 cm (2 in) from one end. Repeat at the other end. (This 'dent' is visible in *fig 2*.)

5 Repeat the above steps on the second cracker.

6 Measure the ends of the crackers and moisten with a little water. Roll out the black sugarpaste (rolled fondant icing). Cut out four circles slightly larger than the ends of the crackers. Stick one circle onto each end.

8 Roll out 200 g (7 oz) of green sugarpaste. Cut out a strip 20 cm x 13 cm (8 in x 5 in). Moisten the centre of the cracker and wind the strip around it. Take a No 3 piping nozzle and press a line of decorative circles along both edges of the strip.

9 Repeat the above procedures on the second cracker, except this time use green sugarpaste for the ends of the cracker and red for the central strip.

10 Pipe small loops along the edges of the central strips using a No 1 nozzle and white royal icing (*fig 3*).

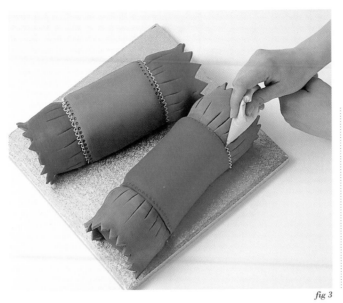

fig 3

11 Pipe a line of small dots around the jagged edges of both crackers.

12 Lift and arrange both crackers on the board using a fish slice (pancake turner).

13 Cut two strips of tartan ribbon approximately 23 cm (9 in) long. Place one diagonally across the central strip of each cracker and secure with a little royal icing.

14 Finally, make two neat bows and stick on the top of each cracker with a little blob of royal icing.

TIP: *If you don't fancy piping around the centres of the crackers, drape some tinsel over the edges instead for a sparkling alternative look. Remove the tinsel before eating.*

GET WELL SOON

There's no prize for guessing the most apt situation this cake is aimed at. But at least bearing down on an ailing friend or relative with this humorous cake would be a bit more original than grapes! Alternatively, stick a few candles around the board and you have the perfect birthday cake for the favourite hypochondriac in your life.

INGREDIENTS

15 cm (6 in) round sponge
1 quantity buttercream (see page 10)
500 g (1 lb 2 oz) flesh-coloured sugarpaste (rolled fondant icing)
50 g (2 oz) black sugarpaste (rolled fondant icing)
20 g (¾ oz) white sugarpaste (rolled fondant icing)
75 g (3 oz) red sugarpaste (rolled fondant icing)
500 g (1 lb 2 oz) green sugarpaste (rolled fondant icing)
10 g (¼ oz) yellow sugarpaste (rolled fondant icing)
20 g (¾ oz) blue sugarpaste (rolled fondant icing)
1 candy stick
Red and black food colours
Icing (confectioners') sugar, for rolling out
Water

UTENSILS

23 cm (9 in) round cake board
Carving knife
Palette knife (metal spatula)
Small sharp knife
Rolling pin
Template for hair (see page 94)
Paintbrushes, one medium, one fine

1 Level the sponge and position it on the cake board. Split it in half and fill the middle with buttercream. Reassemble and spread buttercream around the sides and top.

2 Roll out and cover the cake with 450 g (1 lb) of flesh-coloured sugarpaste (rolled fondant icing). Trim and keep any excess.

3 Knead and roll the black sugarpaste. Cut out a fringe and keep the trimmings, using the template if necessary. Stick this into place with water.

4 Knead and roll out the white sugarpaste. Cut out two circles about 2.5 cm (1 in) in diameter for the eyes.

fig 1

5 Cut out a slightly larger circle out of 10 g (¼ oz) flesh-coloured sugarpaste. Cut this in half and stick one half over each eye (*fig 1*). Add a thin string of black along the base of both eyelids and stick a small flattened circle of black in each eye. Finish off the eyes with two tiny balls of white for the highlights.

6 Make a round nose out of 40 g (2 ½ oz) of flesh-coloured sugarpaste and stick in place.

7 Roll about 5 g (⅛ oz) of black icing into a thin string for a mouth and position this to look miserable.

fig 2

8 Make a thermometer out of a candy stick. Paint a few black marks up the stick and add a thin red line. Finish with a ball of white on the top. Paint a small curved line at the corners of the mouth and insert the thermometer (*fig 2*).

9 Stick a few red sugarpaste spots onto the face.

10 Knead and roll out the green sugarpaste into a strip about 60 cm x 7.5 cm (23 in x 3 in) long. Roll the sugarpaste into a bandage.

11 Moisten side of head and wrap the green sugarpaste round (*fig 3*).

12 Roll out and cut 50 g (2 oz) of red sugarpaste into a rectangle 7.5 cm x 5 cm (3 in x 2 in). Cut the rectangle into a fringe and stick into position on scarf.

13 Finally, add two small stripes. Make one out of blue sugarpaste and the other out of yellow.

TIP: *Rather than using red sugarpaste to make the patient's spots you could use red coloured sweets (candies).*

fig 3

TEMPLATES

HORRIBLE CHILD page 24
enlarge templates by 145%

TEDDY CAKE page 30
enlarge templates by 125%

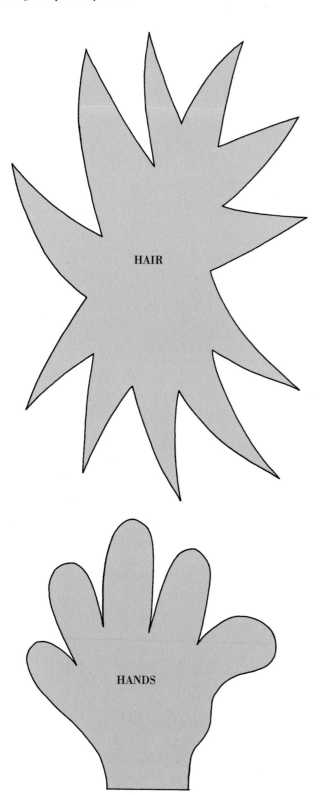

HAIR

HANDS

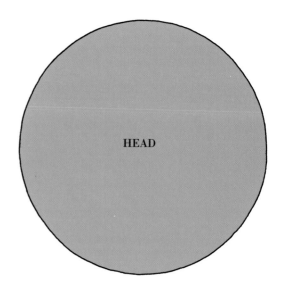

HEAD

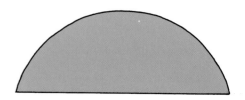

BODY

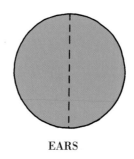

EARS

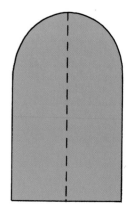

ARMS

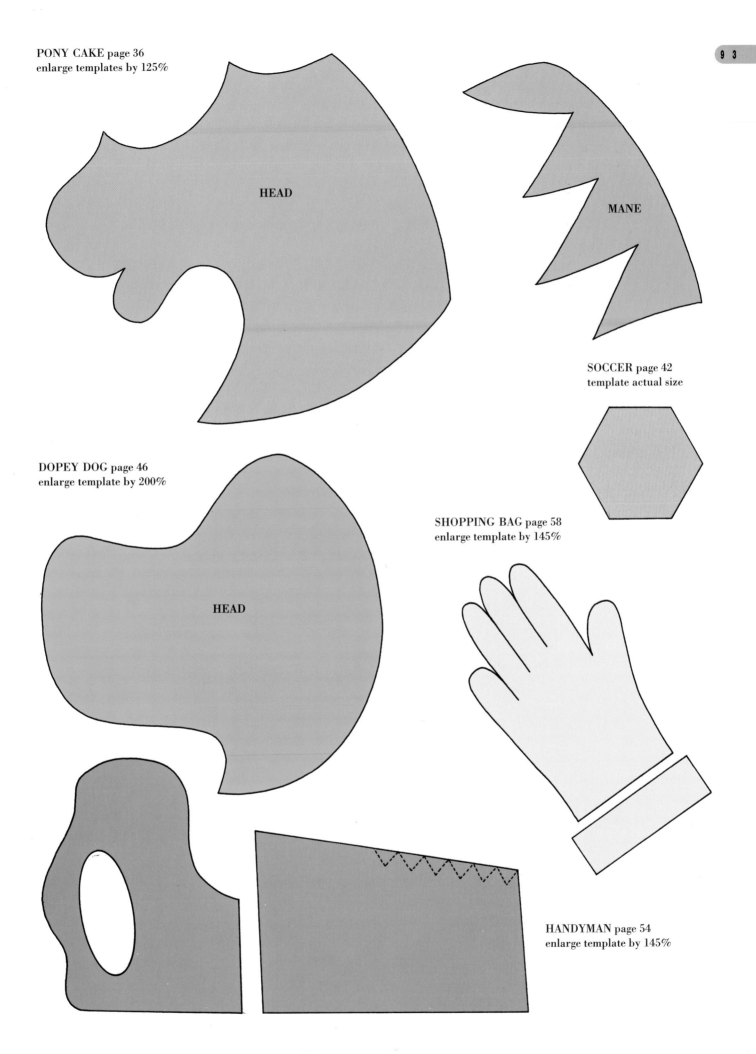

PONY CAKE page 36
enlarge templates by 125%

HEAD

MANE

SOCCER page 42
template actual size

DOPEY DOG page 46
enlarge template by 200%

HEAD

SHOPPING BAG page 58
enlarge template by 145%

HANDYMAN page 54
enlarge template by 145%

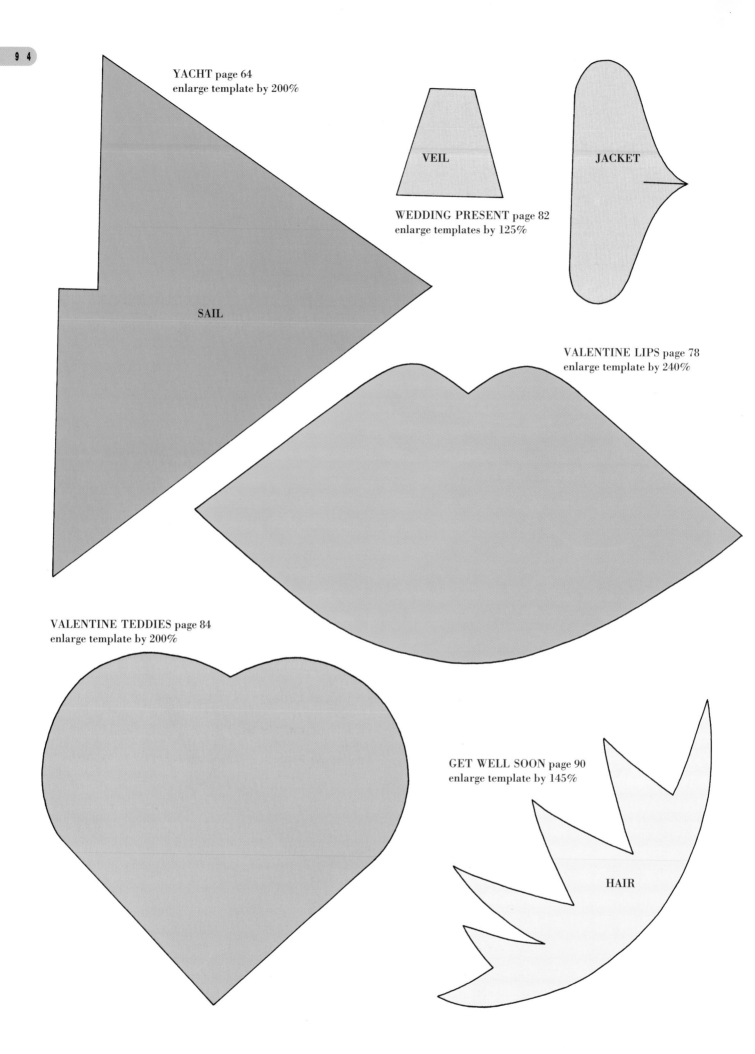

YACHT page 64
enlarge template by 200%

VEIL

JACKET

WEDDING PRESENT page 82
enlarge templates by 125%

SAIL

VALENTINE LIPS page 78
enlarge template by 240%

VALENTINE TEDDIES page 84
enlarge template by 200%

GET WELL SOON page 90
enlarge template by 145%

HAIR

SUPPLIERS

If you have difficulty in obtaining sugarpaste and other cake decorating supplies, including cake tins, try contacting the following companies:

UNITED KINGDOM

J. F. RENSHAW LTD
Crown Street
Liverpool L8 7RF
Tel: (0151) 706 8200

CAKE ART LTD
Venture Way
Crown Estate
Priorswood
Taunton
Somerset TA2 8DE
Tel: (01823) 321532

DIVERTIMENTI
139-141 Fulham Road
South Kensington
London SW3 6SD
Tel: (0171) 581 8065
also at
45-47 Wigmore Street
London W1H 9LE
Tel: (0171) 935 0689

CRAIG MILLAR LTD
Craig Millar House
Stadium Road
Bromborough
Wirral
Merseyside L62 39U
Tel: (0151) 346 1600

SOUTH AFRICA

THE SOUTH BAKELS group is country-wide and supplies to specialist stores as well as the general public. Branches available in the following centres:

P.O. Box 395
Paarden Eiland
Cape Town 7420
Tel: (021) 511 1381

P.O. Box 9583
Johannesburg 2000
Tel: (011) 673 2100

PIETERSBURG
C/o F. M. Marketing
P.O. Box 2365
Pietersburg 0700
Tel: (01521) 73397

EAST LONDON/CISKEI
C/o Bakels
P.O. Box 1187
East London 5200
Tel: (0403) 631 378

BLOEMFONTEIN
C/o Sentraalwes Co-op
P.O. Box 4578
Bloemfontein 9300
Tel: (051) 357 224

NELSPRUIT
C/o Pret-Co Distributors
P.O. Box 3788
Nelspruit 1200
Tel: (01311) 25230

PIETERMARISZBURG
P.O. Box 100671
Scottsville 3209
Tel: (0331) 61340

WINDHOCK
C/o Quality Products
P.O. Box 22242
Windhock 9000
Tel: (061) 228 200

AUSTRALIA

THE CAKE DECORATING CENTRE
1 Adelaide Arcade
Adelaide
South Australia 5000
Tel: (08) 223 1719

FINISHING TOUCHES CAKE DECORATING CENTRE
268 Centre Road
Bentleigh
Victoria 3204
Tel: (03) 223 1719

HOLLYWOOD CAKE DECORATIONS
52 Beach Street
Kogarah
NSW 2217
Tel: (02) 587 153

CAKE AND ICING CENTRE
651 Samford Road
Mitchelton
Queensland 4053
Tel: (07) 355 3443

PETERSEN'S CAKE DECORATIONS
Rear 698 Beaufort Street
Mt Lawley
West Australia 6050
Tel: (09) 271 1692

NEW ZEALAND

DECOR CAKES (WHOLESALE) LTD
17a Queen Street
Otahuhu
Tel: (09) 276 3443

GOLDEN BRIDGE MARKETING LTD
(wholesale)
Cnr Ride Way & William Pickering Drive
Albany
Tel: (09) 415 8777

SUGARCRAFTS NZ LTD
99 Queens Road
Panmure
Tel: (09) 527 6060

THE CAKE STUDIO
3 Mt Eden Road
Mt Eden
Tel: (09) 373 3492

STARLINE DISTRIBUTORS LTD
28 Jessie Street
Wellington
Tel: (04) 385 7424

HITCHON INTERNATIONAL LTD
220 Antiqua Street
Christchurch
Tel: (03) 365 3843

INDEX